Not for the Poor Alone

European Social Services

Alfred J. Kahn and Sheila B. Kamerman

Not for the Poor Alone is about social services for the average citizen, for any citizen. The premise is that ordinary people in the United States are being deprived of constructive solutions to problems in daily living— "normal" problems, that is, ones arising out of societal change. The United States has not faced the fact that social services can serve all people, normal people, and that such services are no less essential to a society than the more traditional public welfare undertakings for the poor and the deviant. In contrast to the view that such social services could undermine the family, could "federalize" the children, this book argues that adequate development of social services is a way of buttressing society and creating community support systems for normal development.

Ten programs for average people in five northern European countries are examined. The technical content was prepared by experts in the countries involved; visiting and observation were carried out by Americans so that the report might be presented "through American eyes."

The book follows the life cycle, going from the newborn to the aged. The focus shifts from health to day care, to school meals, to housing, to home helps, to family vacations, to community support systems for the aged, and to social insurance. There is a broader historical and philosophical context, but much of the book actually involves vivid description and reports of visits, with the end result that the reader comes to understand the philosophy

Not for the Poor Alone

European Social Services

*Alfred J. Kahn
and Sheila B. Kamerman*

TEMPLE UNIVERSITY PRESS
Philadelphia

With the participation of Vera Shlakman, Marianne Kärre, Harriet
Sebag-Montefiore, Françoise Joublin, and Inger Koch-Nielsen

Temple University Press, Philadelphia 19122
© 1975 by Temple University. All rights reserved
Published 1975
Printed in the United States of America

International Standard Book Number: 0-87722-045-X
Library of Congress Catalog Card Number: 75-14690

and quality of the programs from seeing them in action.

Why look at the European perspective on social services? For Europeans, there seem to be fewer ideological stumbling blocks in the way of innovation in social programs. The American system allows special privileges to the rich (tax loopholes) and, along with heavy disadvantages, special services to the poor (the welfare system). European societies tend to take a more comprehensive view of social services and see them as public utilities, which, like energy and education, should be available to all as a matter of course, without shame or excessive idealism.

Of course, no country can adopt another's ideas unchanged. And, indeed, the programs described here are not ideals to be emulated; they are rather vital experiments that are examined in action, with the human consequences fully visible.

ALFRED J. KAHN is project director and and SHEILA B. KAMERMAN is associate director of Cross-National Studies of Social Service Systems at the Columbia University School of Social Work. They have previously collaborated, along with Brenda G. McGowan, on *Child Advocacy*.

Dr. Kahn teaches social policy and social planning at the Columbia University School of Social Work, where he has been a faculty member since 1947. He has written and advised on virtually every aspect of social policy. Most recently, Dr. Kahn has edited *Shaping the New Social Work* and written *Social Policy and Social Services* and two companion volumes, *Theory and Practice of Social Planning* and *Studies in Social Policy and Planning*.

Dr. Kamerman has served as a consultant to government agencies and contributed to numerous journals, especially on the subject of child advocacy.

Contents

Introduction

MANY of the things we Americans do or fail to do, though they can be understood historically, make too little sense for a modern society. Our economy, our communities, our families are changing. Our social policy dare not lag too far behind.

For the poor, Americans expect government to provide some income assistance (public assistance, supplementary security income). We support the idea that government and voluntary social agencies should provide benefits and services for the poor, the troubled, the dependent, the deviant, the disturbed. Some of this support is generous, helpful, and of high quality. Some of it reflects ambivalence, fear, or resentment—and ends by becoming controlling, inadequate, even primitive.

On the other hand, the American government also provides benefits for the rich, the businessman, the relatively fortunate. In this category are mortgage guarantees and real estate loan interest deductions, business expense deductions, and agricultural subsidies.

From one point of view, provisions for the poor and those for the fortunate are obviously different. From another, they both represent benefits and services assigned for important public reasons, in the public interest, and not achieved through marketplace transactions. They are both social welfare activities.

Between the two are some programs—given the broad title "social services" in most of the world but called only by their unique institutional names in the United States—which are assumed to be essential for all people in any modern society. We might list elementary, secondary, and higher education (free or highly subsidized); public health activity; parks and recreational facilities; cultural activities; public employment services. In one vocabulary these constitute the social infrastructure of a complex society. We call them public social utilities. Certainly the public sees them as no less legitimate than water supply, for example, or roads and transportation and communication systems.

Government, business, and voluntary social service agencies are active in all three domains; there is intervention, allocation of tax funds, assignment of personnel. Yet history and ideology have caused us to take one attitude toward public or private welfare services for the poor, another toward subsidy for the affluent, and still another toward public social utilities, or social infrastructure for everyone. Society masks realities by distinguishing among what it calls public welfare and social services for the poor and troubled, education and public health protections for everyone, and benefits for the affluent. It fails to recognize that, in a more basic sense, there are really two categories, not three: social services and benefits connected to problems and breakdowns (and *these* are not limited to the poor), and *social services and benefits needed by average people under ordinary circumstances.*

The price of attitudinal lags in the United States is that the average person, the average family, is constantly deprived in important ways in daily life. The society simply does not do its necessary part, and the consequences are felt by communities, families, and individuals. For this reason, we have written a book about programs and attitudes in several European countries—about services created or assigned by government and the voluntary sector for the average citizen, for *any* citizen. Some explanation is needed, of course, as to why we chose to report on Europe. After all, countries have seldom been able to learn from history —or from one another—deliberately and systematically. In fact, it is unlikely that the institutions or cultural "answers" of one group will work elsewhere, if duplicated in exact form.

But though reproduction in exact detail may not be desirable, exciting social invention may inspire other similar initiatives. European developments seem to be premised on attitudes toward individual needs and governmental responsibility which are at least different from ours— and might be worth discussing for that very reason. Furthermore, societal developments in the United States are accompanied by needs, problems, and requirements which have not yet received adequate attention.

We have reserved for the final chapter the documentation of trends in the society at large and in family life which make new social inventions, new social provision, essential. We are throughout constantly aware of the fact that while there may be widespread intellectual recognition of the fact that family life in the United States needs strengthening, and that supports to traditional and new patterns of primary group living pay off for individuals and for the society, there are inhibitions to action. Our cultural and political traditions say—or are believed by some people to say—that governmental activity in this sphere is probably counterproductive: government interferes, creates dependency, distorts preferences, perhaps inhibits freedom. We Americans are willing to let government act in specific ways for those already "deviant," "dependent," or "failures." Under these latter circumstances, programs are meant to use controls and serve as instruments of desirable change. To create programs for other people, for people not in trouble, is to ensure dependence.

In some European countries people respond to social developments on another premise. At least they seem to want government to do more for individuals in some categories and for families—and apparently have fewer cultural and ideological inhibitions. Some of them say that communal "solidarity" requires some programs, that individuals have a right to expect services, just as a government has a right to expect responsible citizenship and tax payment. The result seems to be less-inhibited social innovation or experimentation in program forms in the social services.[1] Since programs are designed for the typical citizen, for any citizen, not just for the dependent and the cast-offs, programs can be of good quality and need not be demeaning. Limitations that arise stem from limited knowledge and skill, bureaucratic and organizational problems, and resource constraints—not from a cultural fear that social services good enough for anyone will be overutilized and will subvert deeply held values.

At least this is sometimes the response. Europeans, after all, do have some residues of poor law. They have religious traditions and cultural history that affect their views of the respective roles of government and the voluntary sector. They have political ideologies that affect their social welfare philosophies.

Thus, depending on the country, European program development is based on cultural inhibitions that are fewer than, or at least different from, what we know in the United States. The ideological and value

1. Here the term "social services" is used in its broadest international sense to include social sector programming in health, education, housing, income maintenance, and so forth. The comparable U.S. term is "social welfare." Included are benefits, entitlements, services distributed by other than pure marketplace criteria as a result of a mix of governmental and nongovernmental policy and enactment. Within this domain are the "general" or "personal" social services: family and child welfare, services to the aged, home helps, community centers, community care for the emotionally disturbed, school social work, services to adolescents, etc. Where government has a coherent ideology and ties it over time to a series of measures in which family is the criterion of policy or the vehicle to achieve governmental goals, Europeans may use the term "family policy," a term also heard occasionally of late in the United States.

context remains sufficiently different from ours to have created other conceptions of governmental responsibility and different approaches to social services. Sometimes the Europeans strive for a systematic "family policy." It is the purpose of this volume to describe some of these differences. The programs and the attitudes are not all necessarily attractive and appealing but even where they are rejected they can be suggestive. For this is the final item on the list of justifications: Exciting program initiatives and policies are all too rare in our advanced industrial societies. There is desperate need for variation, innovation, experimentation. Exposure to other approaches, different premises, could and should inspire.

With this in view we have not necessarily selected ideal programs or even the best in their fields. In each instance the intent has been somehow to reach the American ethic. Almost any of the topics selected could have been covered in a different country. Almost all the countries visited have other programs of which they are equally or more proud than the ones reported. Like us, almost all are now concerned with inflation and recession, but these concerns do not change their fundamental commitments.

We have followed a method designed in relation to our objectives. European collaborators, who are listed on the copyright page, prepared technical program materials for us (or assembled them where they already existed) and guided us in selecting programs and scheduling visits. They often accompanied the American visitors. The programs were visited by one of us or by our colleague, Professor Vera Shlakman, so that the picture would be presented from the vantage points most relevant to Americans. The report, in short, is offered through American eyes.

Our debt to many people is thus clear: foreign experts and staff of international organizations who helped identify possibilities; government officials who arranged for access, carried out briefings, and offered needed technical materials; foreign colleagues who did much of the work; Professor Shlakman, who visited three types of programs; American experts in the several fields who commented upon our observations; Essie Bailey, Diana Scott, Cynthia Chun, and Winnie Tuthill, who did much to help us to move from visit to visit, then from draft to draft.

Susan Berresford and her colleagues at the Ford Foundation deserve a special acknowledgement. They recognized that the debate about equality of women and the future of the family could, perhaps, be enriched by some information about services for families and other people. This is what we offer here.

Not for the Poor Alone

1

Health Visiting

in England

ALTHOUGH some services for maternal and child health care were provided as early as the mid-nineteenth century, the health-visiting program as it is known in England today began with the passage of legislation in 1936 requiring formal notification of the birth of an infant to the local medical officer of health. Any doctor or midwife witnessing the birth of a child must make such notification within forty-eight hours; if a child is born at home, the parents themselves are required to report the birth within six weeks. Shortly after being notified, the medical officer sends a card, with the parents' name and address, to the health visitor of the area or to the general practitioner in charge of the child's medical care. If the birth occurs in a hospital, the health visitor may initiate the first visit either in the hospital or shortly after mother and child return home. If the birth occurs at home, ten days of midwife care are provided; the health visitor may initiate services during that period, but in any case *must* visit shortly thereafter.

Although mothers may refuse the services of the health visitor, strong efforts are made to complete at least one visit. When deemed necessary by the health visitor and acceptable to the mother, such visiting is continued at regular intervals. In addition, doctors may refer other appropriate cases directly to the health visitor. Finally, if ongoing nursing care or clinical treatment is required, the district nurse is called in.

Although the program was initiated as a mandatory health-screening and reporting system directed toward children up to five years old, in 1948 it began to focus on the whole family. The program is still expanding, and coverage is becoming even more general.

Health visitors are registered nurses who have taken additional specialized training. Most are employed by local health authorities, although some may work for the local department of education as part of the school health service. Outside the rural areas, where she may be midwife and visiting nurse, the health visitor is primarily concerned with providing information, advice, referral, follow-up, advocacy, and some direct service. Much of her work is with mothers and young children, but her duties also include responsibility for the mentally ill in the community as well as for the physically handicapped and the aged. In addition, she is responsible for visiting and supervising child minders (family day-care helpers), nursery schools, and foster homes.

A job description for the position of health visitor states her responsibilities as follows: to give a continuing service to all individuals and families; to make an early assessment, identify needs, and mobilize resources; to promote physical and mental health; and to promote health education. More specifically, as a member of the "primary health team" or what we would call the community health team, her work involves the following professional services, liaison and administrative tasks: (1) periodic home visits to all mothers and children to check developmental progress and social environmental factors; (2) early recognition of deviation from the normal with special emphasis on high risk groups; (3) counseling and participation in child health clinics; (4) health education to individuals and groups in schools and preparation of visual aids, organization of displays, and participation in health education in the sphere of preventive medicine (e.g., early detection of cancer, the prevention of accidents); (5) participation in the school health services as required; (6) support of the elderly and their families and referral, if necessary, to the appropriate agency; (7) supportive visits to the chronically sick, the physically and mentally handicapped, the mentally ill, and their families and contact with other appropriate agencies; (8) support of immigrant families, ensuring that they are aware of the services available; (9) attendance at case conferences; (10) participation in screening procedures; (11) participation in surveys and research; (12) visits in connection with the control of infectious diseases under the direction of the medical officer of health; (13) keeping of adequate records of the amount and type of work carried out and rendering to the nursing office such returns as may be required from time to time; (14) liaison with hospital staff, field workers of the social services department, and workers of other statutory and voluntary agencies, as appropriate.

Regardless of the range of their duties, according to studies most health visitors are kept busy visiting young mothers and children in their homes or in helping at the maternity and child-welfare centers. Indeed, there are few parents who have not come in contact with the health visitor. As of September 30, 1972, there were 8,055 health visitors in England, representing the equivalent of about 6,200 full-time workers. The number is increasing at a rate of about 4 percent per year. Until this year, appointments as health visitors were restricted to women; however, these regulations have now been changed and men are being actively recruited. In 1972 health visitors handled well over four million cases.

Anyone who is caring for a young child, is an expectant or nursing mother, or is suffering from illness, injury, or disability can ask to see the health visitor. Requests for visits tend to be met more rapidly if made by a young or expectant mother. However, efforts are being made to give more attention to the needs of the elderly and the handicapped; some localities have begun to use specialized geriatric visitors who may not be nurses but have received some training specifically related to visiting and advising the elderly.

In one semirural and urban area quite a distance from London, the mother and child focus remains central. Hospitals, general practitioners, and health visitors, buttressed by computer, have created an efficient child-health supervision system. In brief, rosters are printed out to trigger follow-up visits to the house or to invite the mother to visit the office with her child. The visits include immunization services and checkups strategic for that age. If the visit takes place, the computer is notified. If it does not, the health visitor gets the name for a follow-up. There are seven mandated protection points: at eleven days after birth (health visitor, home); at six weeks (health visitor, home); at six months (general practitioner or pediatrician, office); at nine months (health visitor); at two years (pediatrician); at three years (health visitor); and at four years (preschool medical checkup by school medical officer). All social classes are covered. No service is imposed, and citizens may elect their own alternatives. However, this system offers universal coverage and is universally used—all in the context of National Health Service entitlements.

As an illustration of one of the newer developments in the health-visiting program, a special demonstration project devoted to identifying the needs of the elderly and providing services for their care in the community was recently completed in Reading, a mixed manufacturing town a half hour's train ride from London, with a population a little over 100,000. Services to the elderly increased sharply in this area (over 500 percent between 1966 and 1970) when the health visitors began to be attached to the practice of family physicians, working among practice patients instead of in the traditional geographic areas. The family physician—general practitioner—is now the primary source of referral, and all elderly persons referred by him are visited and have their needs assessed by the health visitor, who then takes any action needed, calling upon the appropriate social services and arranging for follow-up visits as required.

At the onset of the program, attempts were made to meet demands as they arose, but there was no systematic method for determining the extent of need among the elderly population as a whole or for establishing priorities for the provision of services. Although geriatric visiting had increased dramatically, referrals were often made too late for preventive action and many old people were still being admitted to institutions for care because health and social services were brought in too late.

A demonstration project implemented in one community in this area was aimed specifically at visiting all people over the age of sixty-five, in order to identify their needs, assess priorities for available public and/or voluntary services, and identify gaps in existing services for the purpose of future planning efforts. Among the anticipated consequences of this study is the increased involvement of health visitors in providing geriatric health services.

A Day with a Health Visitor in London

Southwark, one of London's largest working-class boroughs, is located south of the Thames, on the "other side" of the river. Miss T. is a health visitor serving a part of this inner-city borough. However, to the people who live in the neighborhood surrounding Guy's Hospital, one of London's foremost teaching hospitals, she is *the* health visitor, a well-known figure throughout the community she has served for more than sixteen years. She knows everyone in the neighborhood—the children, their parents and grandparents—and they know her equally well. Mention a name and her incredible memory dredges up an entire life history, without recourse to the bulging records filed away in her office. She knows every house and apartment in the area too. Mention an address, and not only can she lead you unhesitantly to it through the rabbit warrens of streets boasting poetic if inappropriate names, but she can describe the layout with unerring accuracy. Originally trained as a nurse, Miss T. is currently employed by the local health authority and based at the well-baby clinic near the hospital.

According to legislation enacted in 1936, the local government must be notified of every birth that takes place whether at home or in a hospital, and each newborn infant must have at least one statutory visit from a health visitor. Technically, this visit provides the basis for the initial maternal and child-health service provided, and is one of the main sources for new cases and referrals to the health visitor, but in reality it is like a pebble thrown into a pond. As Miss T. explained, the conscientious "HV" looks for the spreading ripples and can find herself visiting the great-grandparents of the newborn as a result of a neighbor's chance comment.

A social worker based for several years at the hospital's child-psychiatry clinic just down the street from the health visitor's office commented that accompanying Miss T. on her neighborhood rounds is like entering a world in which physical disorder and daily crises are the dominant characteristics of ordinary, routine living. Here are families too overwhelmed by the multiple problems inherent in their daily fight for survival to cope with bringing a child to a general practitioner for a referral to the child-guidance clinic. For them, Miss T. provides an essential community outreach service. She visits them in their own homes, bringing information, advice, referral, comfort, help, and advocacy. On occasion, she may even provide a personal escort for a fearful mother or a partial invalid to whatever service may be needed.

We accompanied her on a "typical" day of visiting. Her first stop was at Mrs. W.'s, whose two-room apartment was so dimly lit that we could barely discern the woman's spare, bent frame. Without toilet or bath, Mrs. W. lives here with her five-year-old autistic son. All washing of clothes, dishes, utensils, and bodies is done in the sitting-room sink, so that whatever we did not see, we could certainly smell. At the time of our visit, shortly after 9:30 in the morning, her son was away attending a special day school, arranged after several abortive attempts by Miss T. This large, robust child insists that his mother carry him to the school bus, yet at home he is very aggressive, attacking her physically without any apparent reason, but inevitably if and when she tries to make contact with other people. Until Miss T. was able to expedite his entrance into the special school for maladjusted children, Mrs. W. was almost completely isolated and at her wits' end. Besides being the only social contact this overburdened woman has, Miss T. now acts as a link between Mrs. W. and her son's teacher. A current problem was that the boy refused to put on his new school clothes, clinging stubbornly to the worn-out shreds of other clothes, long since outgrown. Mrs. W.

is still too timid, too fearful that somehow the boy will not be permitted to remain at the school, to ask the teacher's help. So Miss T. offered to discuss the problem with the teacher, to see if she can help. Similarly, she will discuss the mother's anxiety and concerns with school staff, so that the school will be more understanding and knowledgeable about the child.

On the way to the second visit, we passed the burned-out apartment of the A. family. Mrs. A. was out when the fire started, but her three young children were home. Miraculously, neighbors sounded the alarm in time for all three to be rescued. Temporarily rehoused, Mrs. A. lives with her guilt and with the neighbors' contempt for what they see as her irresponsible behavior. She considers the health visitor her "only friend," and Miss T. understands. We stopped briefly, to visit and chat. On leaving, Miss T. told us that Mrs. A.'s husband had left her: "She has no family nearby, and she's only a young child herself, needing an occasional night out and not intentionally neglectful of her children."

Miss T. has little patience with cultural differences when they seem to her to lead to problems for children. Thus, she feels free to be blunt and forthright in advising mothers that "fostering out" their children to families in the country is not good practice. In explaining the intensity of her feeling, she says that she sees clearly the effect on a generation of mothers who were evacuated in their early childhood and separated from their mothers during World War II. Deprived themselves of adequate mothering, they have little to give their children; nor can their own or their children's emotional needs be better met by husbands who have undergone similar deprivation.

Our third visit was to the D.'s apartment. Six years ago, Mr. D. found Sylvie, a slight, sweet girl in her early twenties, wandering the streets. Taking her home with him, feeding and clothing her, he subsequently discovered that she had recently been discharged from an institution for educationally subnormal youngsters, and that she had been diagnosed as retarded with an IQ of 68. Twenty years her senior, he became her protector—half father, half lover. They have one little girl, aged three and a half, who was just beginning to talk when the authorities placed her in an institution for neglected children, following a wild party to which the police turned up as uninvited guests. Miss T. has known the family since the birth of the child, and considers the home a loving one, albeit unconventional. She fought the authorities, documenting her position with personal knowledge and written records going back almost four years. Finally, she managed to have the child returned to her parents, but by then the child had lost all speech. Miss

T. continues to view the family as her personal responsibility, and this visit was to complete arrangements for providing speech therapy for the child.

Our next visit was to an Indian family, Mr. and Mrs. L., who have six children, all at school except the four year old, who goes only half-days. Mrs. L. has a hearing loss, but steadfastly refuses to wear the aid Miss T. obtained. Her husband, who was at home, complained that since her recent operation she talks constantly to unseen companions. She countered by accusing him of drunken, abusive behavior and jealous rages. He said that she makes impossible financial demands on him, yet he produced a payslip that was not consistent with the obvious material discomforts of the home. The four year old and the ten year old, home during his school lunch hour and en route to take the family clothes to the local launderette, were fascinated by the whole exchange. Mrs. L. complained of stomach pains, pointing to a distended belly that looked as if she were pregnant once more. Miss T. told her to go to the doctor's clinic that afternoon for an examination and also suggested (and subsequently arranged for) family counseling.

Finally, we stopped to see a West Indian girl, at nineteen not much more than a child herself, but the mother of a premature baby still in the hospital, a three-year-old boy who bounces in and out of foster homes at his mother's whim, and an appealing eighteen-month old girl who is reproached by her mother for behaving "like a baby." Miss R. wants her baby home from the hospital, but in the next ambivalent breath admitted to feeling tired and tense. Miss T. functions as a communications service in this household as well as in many others in this largely telephoneless community. She will carry Miss R.'s message back to the medical staff at the hospital, and will later tell Miss R. the day the doctors are ready to discharge her baby. By the time we left, after extensive discussion, Miss R. had agreed that she was not yet ready to cope with the infant. On departure, Miss T. commented somewhat helplessly and unhappily to us that she is afraid Miss R. may never be.

As we moved from street to street, Miss T. stopped to chat with many of her acquaintances. She picked up a great deal of information informally and dispensed much needed advice. Many of these chance encounters result in visits to the clinic later in the afternoon, following Miss T.'s suggestions. And at the clinic she is available for all kinds of additional assistance. Technically, this is a well-baby clinic, for children under five, but in addition to those receiving their periodic checkups, a stream of sick children turn up whose mothers trust the clinic more than any other facility in the area. A forty-year-old chronic schizophrenic, long known to Miss T., wandered in for employment advice; a young girl, whom Miss T. has known since infancy, asked for information about contraceptive devices. In between, Miss T. explained the techniques for burping newborns to puzzled young mothers. She had already supplied this information during the antenatal clinics she conducts twice weekly, but inevitably some women never bother to turn up until faced with a colicky, crying infant.

Around the corner from the waiting room, all sorts of baby preparations are dispensed at cost. Originally this service was a way of ensuring attendance at the clinic. Now the supermarkets offer more competitive prices than the small neighborhood shops ever could, yet the service continues in this neighborhood, where mothers place so much confidence in the health visitor's recommendations.

After two or more hours in the clinic, depending on the volume of patients, Miss T. will stop at the nearby Children's Hospital and visit patients on the obstetrics ward, before catching her train for home. During these in-patient visits, she will collect material for the following day's neighborhood rounds.

The story of Miss T. is neither typical nor atypical; the program is in flux. In fact, the British describe their health-visiting service—home visiting of families and individuals by specially trained registered nurses —as a program in transition. Almost every industrialized country has initiated some kind of mandatory health screening for children, but the British version is now being expanded to cover services for the elderly, the physically handicapped, and the mentally ill living in the community. One London borough where we spent some time with the health visitor at the local clinic provides among other services a free domiciliary (home visiting) family-planning service, with visits made jointly by both health visitor and doctor, who give information, advice, and service to both mother and father. From an initial maternal and child-health service, the British are trying to turn the program into one major component of a community-based family-health service.

Despite the problems inherent in any such change, both the care service and the newer expanded coverage are of interest to the American observer for several reasons. Increasing concern in the United States with the need for early identification of developmental problems of young children, coupled with the absence of any coherent program for accomplishing this, has stimulated interest in how other countries approach the problem. Similarly, growing interest in helping the elderly or handicapped live in their own homes, rather than in institutions, requires a new perspective on the panoply of services needed to achieve this.

Whether for family planning or for other purposes, the need for home-related services was stressed wherever we went. Such services provide an essential link to isolated mothers—those who may never venture beyond the corner grocery shop or are even afraid of leaving the house, for example, or those struggling with too many children and too little money who find that something always interferes with a projected visit to the clinic despite good intentions. Moreover, home visiting provides an essential base for the possible identification of abused or neglected children, a problem of increasing concern both in England and in the United States. One health visitor stressed that case finding done informally, in the course of routine visits and a universally provided service, is far more effective and less threatening than any other method of identifying such problems.

In addition, one clinic operates a nursery for short-time relief for mothers and children with special needs and also provides examination rooms for midwives and well-baby supervision. Here, the health visitors do not wait for physician referrals, but build up new baby registrations either by personal contact or through direct access to doctors' records. As elsewhere, mothers may ask the health visitor to call. The staff emphasized the fact that the service is used by all social classes; it has been said that the health visitor would call at Buckingham Palace in the event of the arrival of a baby. Naturally, continued and repeated visiting is neither automatic nor mechanical; service and scheduling are based on assessment of relative needs and requirements in light of health considerations and family condition.

The value of postnatal visiting by the health visitor prior to discharge from the hospital is stressed everywhere. It facilitates identification of tensions, anxieties, and fears; it may prevent postpartum depressions; and it prepares the way for later home-based visits. Initiating such visits at the hospital is particularly effective because it is done at a time when mothers are receptive and need reassurance that support will be available and forthcoming.

Some Facts and Figures

A 1969 survey of the work of the health visitors in London revealed that of the more than a thousand health visitors in the city, about 80 percent worked, as Miss T. does, in a simple geographic area based on a clinic. In the central city area especially, most of this visiting is done on foot; walking around the neighborhood helps the visitor maintain personal contact with the community. Each day, approximately twenty-four thousand people (individuals or family units) received this service in London, and of these, about 30 percent were served at home ("domiciliary" visiting), 40 percent during clinic sessions, 10 percent in consultation with other staff, and the remainder elsewhere, for instance in the office or even over the telephone.

The most frequently served people were children—nearly ten thousand each day, representing 30 percent of the total group. Not far behind (31.2 percent) were mothers and infants up to their first birthday (beyond that age the baby is treated as a separate person). Service to the elderly was infrequent (slightly more than 2 percent of the population served); however, it has increased since then, and there is growing pressure for it to become a more important component of the current program.

Approximately eighteen hundred new contacts are initiated each day in London, representing an average of a little less than two new cases per day for each health visitor. And most of the contacts are made either at home or at the local clinic. Child management or child care is the focus of most visits, with medical screening, general health problems, and immunization of somewhat lesser importance. Among other subjects for which information and advice are requested are financial, legal, and housing problems, mental-health problems, and questions regarding family planning. The range of service provided is extensive, and the need for service is high; as a result, the pressure on the health visitor is substantial. According to the 1969 report, controlling and planning the most effective use of skills and time is a crucial part of the work of the health visitor.

One comment on the British program is necessary to place our visits in proper context. In the past, most health visitors were assigned to a particular geographic area or neighborhood, visiting every infant and mother living there shortly after childbirth. Current British policy is for the health visitor to be assigned to a particular general practitioner, visiting anyone referred for service by the physician responsible for that patient's care.[1] This change in policy is part of the overall pressure to expand service beyond that supplied to mother and child. The program

1. Under the system of health care in the United Kingdom, each person elects a general practitioner who provides ongoing preventive and clinical care and refers to specialists.

in London continues to reflect the earlier neighborhood approach, but outside London, attachment to the practice of the family physician or general practitioner predominates. Our visits were selected to illustrate these variations. We have described visits with a health visitor in London; we will now describe the alternative, newer, and increasingly prevalent approach employed by most health visitors outside London.

A Day with a Health Visitor in East Sussex

A different kind of day, accompanying another health visitor, was spent in an East Sussex community. This is an affluent, exurbanite community, with high land values and small, charming towns, containing spacious and comfortable middle-class homes. Rounds were made with two of the newer breed of health visitors—attractive and lively women in their middle thirties who exuded competence and self-assurance as they visited a variety of homes throughout the community. Although Mrs. A. and Mrs. M. are based in an area nursing office, they are considered to be "attached" to a general practice. At present, more than 70 percent of the health visitors in England follow this pattern, which is currently highly favored by the government and is increasing rapidly. It is anticipated that attachment to general practice will expand the geriatric and disability case load, among other things, even though maternal and child health will continue to be the core concern.

The first visit, routine and anticipated but unannounced, was to Mrs. T. and her newborn infant. The home itself was obviously comfortable and well equipped, the young mother well dressed in a tweed skirt and sweater. Since this was a first child, Mrs. A. began with a fairly lengthy conversation with the mother, exploring how she was feeling and how she was managing with the baby. She stressed the importance of following prescribed exercises to tighten up the mother's abdomen, discussed the infant's feeding schedule, measured the baby's head and examined its skin, navel, limbs, and hips. She said that she would drop by later in the day to leave some special dusting powder for the navel and set up an appointment at the clinic for both mother and child. Although supplies are not invariably provided, they are almost always offered when the child is a first-born. In addition, local practice is to provide disposable diapers if, for example, there is a handicapped child imposing an extra burden on the mother.

Our next stop was at an obviously prosperous home—large, well furnished, and excellently equipped. The visit was to a two-year-old boy who was believed to have suffered brain injury through oxygen deprivation at birth. He was now being cared for by a foster parent, Mrs. G., a woman in her middle forties with a husband and teenage children. The boy had been placed by a neighboring social service department, and the Sussex health visitor was calling because the child was now in her territory. Some months earlier, when he had arrived, David had been inert, but now he was lively and active, though perhaps not too tolerant of frustration. Mrs. A. examined him and played with him for a while, and gradually he responded. Subsequently, she discussed his progress with Mrs. G. and also observed for herself the child's balance, walking, use of hands, color perception, use of toys, and coordination. Although David still showed no signs of speech, he was clearly receiving a great deal of attention and care from his foster mother. Ordinarily, the boy would probably not have been visited at this point, but children with known problems receive more extensive visiting.

Following this, we went to visit a three month old, the second child of a young mother, Mrs. W. The stop was occasioned by the report of possible mild convulsions, which would call for immediate and close observation of the child. Mrs. A. spent some time discussing the symptoms and feeding problems with the mother, but even more time discussing the baby's three-year-old brother (not seen), who had developed behavior problems since the birth of the new infant. It was apparent that Mrs. W. was greatly concerned, and Mrs. A. took time to discuss the problem and to advise her about handling the child.

Our fourth visit was to a large and very prosperous farm to see Mrs. L. and her young twins, one of whom was thought to be lagging developmentally. We did not see the children; they were sleeping, and Mrs. L. was fearful of waking them. She was tense, with the thin, wiry look of someone accustomed to hard manual work. She was the wife of the farmer's son, and until recently, she, her husband, her father-in-law, and his domineering common-law wife had all lived together. After some struggle with depression, however, she had put her foot down and insisted upon moving out of the big house. Now she was beginning to feel much better. She showed us her new home, which was quite beautiful and built in one wing of a stone stable located some few hundred feet from the main house. The house was crammed full with valuable antique furniture, which Mrs. L. had to keep in a high state of polish even while she was fully occupied with the care of her two new infants and a variety of other household duties, including cooking and working in the garden. Mrs. A. congratulated her on her new home, and she responded that it was fine to be on their own. Here, too, Mrs. A. provided her with a great deal of support and reassurance in her growing independence; it was obvious that the family situation was one with which the health visitor was quite familiar. After some time spent on family problems generally, the discussion shifted to the twins. Mrs. A. reminded the mother that it was time for their immunizations, an earlier routine notice to appear having been disregarded because of minor illness. (Immunization notices and reminders of missed appointments are sent out routinely, either by manual clerical operation or by computer.) Mrs. A. explained that a follow-up card would arrive setting another appointment, but if it were easier for the mother, she might disregard it and bring the boys in at her own convenience. After some discussion, a specific appointment was made.

Next, we joined with the local district nurse, who was on her way to change a dressing on the ulcerated leg of an old man living alone in his family farmhouse. Mrs. A. explained that this was a fairly routine visit, to see how Mr. P. was getting along. While driving to the farm, she told us that on a recent visit the old man had been in an angry mood, threatening to take his shotgun to "trespassers'; on our arrival, however, he welcomed us very pleasantly. His dressing was changed, and everyone, including the patient, was pleased with his progress. He was in an amiable mood, and obviously enjoyed being visited by the three of us. Mrs. A., in an aside, asked the district nurse whether the man had adequate income and was assured that he was quite well off. She also questioned how he managed, considering his isolation, and was assured that neighbors helped with the marketing. Mr. P. brought out family photographs to show us, announced his age as eighty-seven, and spent some time reminiscing about the countryside and community in his youth. It was apparent that he had few visitors, and the opportunity to talk with the health visitor and the district nurse was a rare and important opportunity for socializing.

Our last home visit for the day was to Mrs. R., a woman of about sixty living alone in a comfortable house but badly crippled. She had undergone orthopedic surgery for the insertion of a support plate. The operation had left her knee stiff, but would enable her to get about a little with the aid of crutches and cane and thus have some mobility in the house. Mrs. A. wanted to see how she was progressing, partly because of a problem with an old, incompetent neighbor whose cats relieved themselves in a basement common to Mrs. R.'s house; this resulted in fierce and penetrating odors and consequent complaints from Mrs. R. Removing the cats would precipitate a crisis for their owner, but the present situation created grave discomfort for Mrs. R. In the discussion that ensued, though the problem was not resolved, we learned that the district nurse had been in regularly to help her bathe, that a homemaker came in every day to tidy up, and that someone from the local social service office had called the preceding day. In addition, she was now waiting to have a telephone installed. The array of services was impressive, and her capacity to utilize them equally so.

After a brief lunch, we visited the community hospital, part of the local health service but built by community subscription. A small, pleasant general hospital, it does some orthopedic and general surgery and has a delivery room and small four- to six-bed wards, all of which were occupied. Mrs. A. stopped to see one of the patients in the geriatric ward, maintaining that this was part of her regular routine. In the ward were long-stay patients, one of whom was in his late sixties and had been confined to bed here for thirteen years. Although this type of case was certainly not what the hospital was intended to serve, people from the community are kept in a local facility such as this when possible.

Next we visited a local primary school, where the health visitor is responsible for school health education. Here we spent some time with a class of eight year olds, and Mrs. A. discussed with one of the teachers the possibility of a home visit with regard to one of the students. Back at the local clinic, we ended our visit with a brief period observing the weekly antenatal clinic, followed by the regular daily conference with the general practitioner regarding new referrals to the health visitor.

In Perspective

Unquestionably the role of the health visitor in England has changed substantially over the past twenty years. Originally, antenatal and child care, the prevention of home accidents, and advice on immunization, diet, hygiene, and infectious diseases were the services most stressed. Today, the health supervision of children under school age, the early assessment and developmental screening of young children, especially those at special risk, and the provision of liaison between home, school, and hospital continue to be of major concern, but many other types of services are now receiving increased attention. For example, service to the chronically sick, disabled and handicapped, the mentally ill, and the frail and elderly living in the community is a growing component of the job of health visitor. Furthermore, advice on family planning, certain aspects of cancer testing, information, advice, and referral regarding drug abuse, alcoholism, and venereal disease, and the identification of abused and battered children all require attention and service. A recent report on new trends in community health and nursing services emphasized that, in order to achieve maximum impact, it will continue to be necessary to provide most of these services in the home on a personal basis.

With growing stress being placed on providing care in the community, health visiting may well become the core of a community-based health service and family care support program, acting as a link between home and family, on the one hand, and school, clinic, and hospital, on the other. Its boundaries and linkages with what the British call "personal social services" offered by local departments of social work are in the process of much-needed delineation. Some rivalry exists but does not interfere with program growth.

Our American services in this field encompass a tradition of voluntary-sector health visiting to the poor, in some places going back to nineteenth-century charities; city, county or state public-health nursing, in some places mostly for the poor and offering only spotty coverage, but occasionally comprehensive and excellent; and a generally poor system of coverage for everyone. There are home health services, severely limited, at best, and available only on a means-tested basis to the poor, on a high fee-paying basis to the wealthy, or on the basis of physician referral from hospital or nursing home for the aged. We lack what is so central to the British system: routine coverage service for everyone, ensuring a contact after a child is born. This valuable policy, which does not impose service, does guarantee that case finding is undertaken early by a community representative. If there is a handicap or defect, a housing problem, a situation endangering infants, a need for help, someone has the responsibility for discovery and action. In the United States we are only now struggling to implement a 1967 congressional mandate for Early Periodic Diagnosis and Screening (EPDS) for poor children. We are having difficulty, we cannot get coverage, we do not have assurance that case finding will be followed by corrective action, because there is no operating service system and no basis for continuous eligibility. Service is limited to poverty-level children—in so far as it is federally mandated—even though millions of working-class and lower-middle-class children are in urgent need of health supervision and treatment protections. For all our debate about the future of our health service systems, it is far from certain that any likely reform will provide us with these elementary protections.

2

Daytime Care of Young Children

in Sweden

UNDER a variety of names and administrative auspices, and with a diversity of goals, the daytime care of young children away from their own homes is expanding. The Swedish program described in this chapter cannot be called unique, since many of its features have been tried by imaginative people in experimental programs in many places—including some American communities. Yet the Swedish program deserves attention: it is exciting as evidence that a high level of programing and imagination can be sustained over many local jurisdictions. Much of this is accomplished through leadership, encouragement, and technical-financial aid from central authorities and commissions who do not have formal prerogatives with reference to local programing.

Sweden is small (population, 8 million), and relatively homogeneous ethnically and racially. Thus, it cannot be a true model for the United States. However, it is the country closest to us in per-capita income, is exposed to similar child-development and social-policy theories and values, and is applying intelligence to the design of sound programs. It is preoccupied with and constantly debating the shape of preschool programs in the context of a social policy which would actively promote complete equality of the sexes at work, at home, and in child-rearing. Swedish programs are attractive to the American visitor, while raising some very difficult questions which we, too, must answer.

After years of debate and development, Swedish officials have arrived at the following definitions:

Child centers is used as a blanket term covering *day nurseries* (five or more hours per day), or what we would call all-day care; *part-time groups*, called play schools until recently (usually three hours per day); and *free-time centers*, providing before- and after-school care for school-age children. If the free-time program is included with the day nursery and part-time group, the term *joint child center* is usually employed. Children served range from six months to seven years old, the school-entering age.

Preschool is the uniform program term for either day nurseries or part-time groups (play schools). The categorical program differences between these have been ended. The only difference between them is whether the care is all-day or part-day. For infant groups the recommended age spread is six months to two-and-a-half years; for "sibling groups" (see below) it is two and a half to seven.

Small day nurseries serve six to twelve children in a modest facility with trained staff, unlike the day nurseries, which have more elaborate facilities and programs, several groups, and more structured staff patterns.

Family day care is home-based, but supervised and paid. It is a universally familiar program and still a major one in Sweden.

In addition, while administrative responsibilities for them are distributed to several bureaus, Swedish authorities have developed the concept of *complementary preschool activities* to cover such programs as care of ill children for brief periods by child minders on the public payroll (if both parents work), organized park play (which permits children to be dropped off for some hours), and alternatives to preschool for eligible children unable to attend for such reasons as physical handicap and mental retardation or hospitalization for illness. Visiting preschool staff and play therapists are employed for these purposes.[1]

All these programs are guided, supervised, and funded by local governmental authorities, with considerable help and leadership from central government.

In current American discussion, advocates of expanded day care reflect varied objectives: they want to free "welfare" mothers to work, maximize choices for women, enrich socialization of all children, repair cognitive deficits for deprived children, provide custodial all-day or after-school care for children of working mothers, and so forth. Sweden has had good economic reasons in recent decades to want to increase the labor-force participation of its women and thus has needed more day-care resources. However, strong elements in trade unions and politi-

---

1. Mention should also be made of the "playotheques," special "open play schools" for children with mental or physical handicaps, where they are given individual or small-group training by special staff. Such playotheques are now established by each county in Sweden. There are at present about sixty, most of them started and run by parent organizations.

cal leadership also argue that—economic pressures aside—labor-force participation for women is essential to true equality of the sexes. If women are to have freedom to work even when their children are young, day care is an essential resource. Moreover, Swedish social policy leaders in this field have concluded that participation in soundly conceived preschool programs, especially group programs, is also good for children, indeed better than other arrangements. Thus, expansion is planned and continues.

Sandviken and the Commission's Reforms

Sandviken, a city of 90,000 on Sweden's northeast coast, has implemented major national recommendations for preschool pedagogical reform.[2] The basic proposal is that children's groups in day nurseries and part-time programs (all-day and part-day care in the United States) should be "age-mixed' and should be called *sibling groups*. Moreover, the children should have maximum freedom to choose playmates, materials, and objects of study or interest. Each preschool group should have its own two "home rooms" for meals, quiet activity, and rest. The three or four groups in each center would then share one very large, high, central "activity and experiment" hall. The "home room" sibling groupings, which include children of all the eligible ages (two and a half to seven), might then be reconstituted in the large room according to the children's preferences. The size of the room allows a wide range of equipment for very active indoor play when children cannot go out. Indeed, there are also special equipment recommendations in the national report.

Sandviken's Björksätra (Birch Hill) day nursery finds that only the toddlers (two and a half) want a relatively closed-off "home room" setup, and even they sometimes wander out to the older group or are joined by older children. The mixing of age groups seems to work out naturally in this facility, which houses one toddlers' group of eleven children aged two to two and a half and two "sibling" groups, each with seventeen children aged three to seven. The toddlers' group has the

2. For the theory and philosophy and for a summary of the report of the Commission on Child Centres, see Bodil Rosengren, *Pre-School in Sweden* (1973), available through The Swedish Institute in Stockholm and various Swedish offices abroad. The Swedish Institute also issues articles about present developments in its *Current Sweden* reprint series. The Swedish Institute may be addressed at Box 7072, 103–82 Stockholm 7, Sweden.

usual Swedish ratio of one adult to four children (here, one child nurse and two preschool teachers). For the two sibling groups there are four preschool teachers, trainees, or nurses, a ratio of one adult to five children. (Actually, the recommended group size is twenty to twenty-two; some centers over-register to compensate for "normal" absence rates.)

Björksätra is located in a beautiful low building of grayish-brown brick, a pleasant surprise to one who has just heard that this is essentially an average working-class area and that the public treasury is not exceptionally prosperous. When outlining this "new town in town" proposal, the town planners argued that it was long-term economy. The center is on a beautifully landscaped plot close to high-rise residences. To the left of the central entrance hall is a service wing for the kitchen, supply rooms, and a staff meeting room. The corridor ahead leads to the preschool facilities for the three groups and the large central activity room. A paneled corridor beyond the service wing affords similar space to an elementary school.

The outdoor play area is quite wonderful. The equipment is built with thick logs. There is a cabin and storage space and the usual climbing apparatus and swings. When this large development was built, the planners made an attempt—exceptional here because of cost problems—to preserve the landscape, including the trees. Staircases have therefore been constructed on one side of the hill, with slides down the other. Although their "philosophy" calls for admitting neighborhood children to the play area, problems of insurance and liability have forced them to reserve the area to the preschool children.

The director, an impressive, sensitive, firm, imaginative woman with a rich background in the preschool field ("early childhood education" in the United States), was taken on as consultant for the four units in the area which are attempting the new approach. After a while she decided that she preferred direct work in the center as director. Her relationships to the children are of high quality. She is firm, yet warm, and obviously knows them and has a very clear philosophy. Basically the curriculum is English "preschool." Staff are trying to help the children to develop individually, at their own paces, and to find activities appropriate to their own needs.

Home-room space has been set up to include quiet areas where children may sleep if they wish. Most of this space is used for television and quiet small-group activity.

One quality of the facility we noted was that there is never a sense of crowding or of great noise. Walking in, one sees very few children. In almost three hours in this facility, we seldom had four or five children in view at any one time, except when each of the groups went to its own room to eat, usually at two round tables.

During the play periods, the place is full of activity in every room. The children spread themselves naturally all over the place, busy in small, concentrated working groups. One of the light, spacious rooms is equipped with building material for "creative building," another for "sitting" activities—puzzles, intellectual games, small handicrafts. A third room is set up for painting, clay modeling, and other artistic work. In one corner, in a carpentry alcove, a young blond teacher was working with two children, a boy and a girl. The girl was wearing a series of attachable plastics which encompassed her completely, forming something like an airplane, as she shuffled along. She wore this costume for the two hours, including lunch, that we observed her. The little boy was actually concentrating with the teacher on the drilling. This room also contains the miniature kitchen we found to be a standard detail in all Swedish preschools and day nurseries. One room is a marvelous "water play room" where the smaller children were happily playing naked with water and finger paint. Another of the smaller rooms is equipped with science materials for "laboratory" experiments, rather exceptional equipment even for Swedish day nurseries, but now strongly recommended. One boy was riding a bicycle up and down the entry corridor, not in any class area. Another was proudly pushing a wagon.

In one small alcove of a home room, ringed with mattresses, there is a space for quiet play and sleep, but nobody was there until after lunch. Then, at quiet time, a small group followed the teacher in and watched as she adjusted the television set to a children's educational program. Several watched restfully, while one covered himself with a blanket and seemed to sleep. Two others took children's books and turned the pages as they glanced from time to time at the television. The teacher sat in the center with them and watched, but it was quiet and restful.

From any of the rooms, through windowpanes in the walls or doors, one can easily see the central hall. This is a large hall with a lowered ceiling, lit by daylight from the roof windows and full of exciting play material: swings, ladders, climbing nets, all hanging from the low ceiling, and on the floor, thick foam-rubber mattresses for jumping. Even here, there was a quiet group sitting on a secluded "hill" while a teacher showed them a book. Some children were having a great time in here, while others were sitting busily engaged in a game around a table in the next room. In the "building room" two boys were concentratedly busy constructing a railway landscape with wooden rails. They had closed the door with the latchkey. A male teacher, the only one in this center, was with five year olds.

All material is arranged very carefully beforehand. And each box or drawer or cupboard is marked so that the teachers and the children themselves know exactly where to find things. Even a three year old can find the exact item needed at the moment since a specimen of the material inside is pasted on the outside of the drawer.

At noontime each of the groups goes to its "dining room." The distances are large, since the central play area is between them, and we were hardly aware of the fact that three different groups were having lunch. The food is brought in on a wagon from the service area by the cook. In this instance, all the cooking is done at the school. It is a full meal—liver, potatoes, vegetables, milk, bread and butter. (They save the dessert for a later snack, having discovered that the children do not eat dessert at this time.) The children take turns taking out the tableware and setting the table. They seem to learn counting as they check how many things of each kind are needed and how many are missing. At least two teachers, and in one instance three, sit with each group of fifteen. They eat with the children. If a child does not want to eat or to sit, he is free not to. One boy stayed out in the general play area, but since the dining room door was closed, the mealtime was quiet and restful. For the first ten minutes or so the children concentrated quietly on the meal, and everybody seemed to eat. When we commented on the boy who had stayed outside, whom we could see going back and forth on a swing, the director remarked, "We have never seen a child actually starve here." (Later, in discussion, we learned that this child is in many ways disturbed and that there has been discussion with the mother, but no real referral or intensive follow-up has been made other than a considerate handling by the staff here.)

After about ten minutes, a boy got up, apparently not enjoying the meal, and joined the other playing. Then gradually, after about twenty-five minutes, the children drifted out, having carried their plates to the proper place. Some of them immediately resumed very active play, but the others soon assembled with the one teacher in the quiet television room. Of these thirty children in the sibling groups, only one or two actually napped—quite a departure from usual practice elsewhere in Sweden or in other countries. The children arrive at 8:00 for the most part, but some come as early as 6:30. Many leave at 5:00, some at 4:00. The day nursery finds that most of those over three do not need to nap. Moreover, the parents feel that naps during the day interfere with normal sleeping hours at night.

After lunch, one teacher in each group takes major responsibility for the cleanup that remains after the children have done their part. She sponges the table, piles all the rest of the dishes on a cart, and wheels it back to the cook's area. In general, the school has a rather special attitude toward cleanup: all the maintenance work and cleaning is done during the day, in the presence of the children, so they may get a sense of various roles and of the real world. They join in this work, and they also cook.

The nursery school (play school, part-time group) for four to six year olds in the same building has two three-hour sessions, one in the morning and one in the afternoon, for twenty children each, with one teacher and two trainees. Three of the older children at a time are permitted to go to the play hall and join the younger group; over three can cause a problem. Similarly, the little ones may wander in here if they wish for a variation in the day's routine. The arrangement here, too, offers quiet places.

We went to have lunch with the director in a small staff dining room. A little girl who joined the day nursery rather late in the program season, and who consequently tends to follow the director, sat down and wanted to eat with us. That was considered acceptable; it happens once in a while with an individual child. She is well behaved, does not disturb, and lets the general discussion go on. In general, staff allow many children special privileges with adults, but balance it out in the long run. Thus, for example, they believe that a trip should be for two, three, or four children in private cars. On such occasions, they promise the others that they will go on subsequent trips and always keep the promise.

In the luncheon discussion, the director indicated that the transition to this new pattern has been successful from her point of view. What does the shift mean? First, it is felt that the change to sibling groups and away from homogeneous age grouping encourages children to cooperate rather than to compete. Furthermore, there is less attention to "group as group." They are actually working with the children individually in a group setting, they believe. Each child has his or her own program. They believe that the children are less nervous and, as a result, that there is less conflict and aggression requiring intervention.

In general, the staff seems enthusiastic about program and facilities. A more traditional staff would consider this a disordered and unstructured place, but it does not seem very radical or unfamiliar to those acquainted with innovative centers in the United States.

In an attempt to get closer to the parents, they avoid the usual evening meetings and manage brief individual conversations once or twice a term. They are also strict about maintaining a transition period when a child enrolls during which one of the parents or a close relative is present; if the parents' work schedules intervene, enrollment is postponed until a work holiday. If parents can, they join the child for an occasional meal.

Each staff team finds time daily for a conference to discuss what is going on and what plans need to be made. At the beginning, or as new staff is taken on, the cooking staff and cleaning people take part. Later, the conference time is devoted to program planning. Those in charge of the toddlers' group meet while the children sleep. Others confer during periods of play, with the director sometimes filling in. She joins the conference as needed. In general, a good deal of teamwork is required to provide coverage and fair allocation of tasks during the long program days. Staff arrivals are staggered in relation to the arrival times of children at 6:30, 7:30, or 8:30 A.M.

The Sandviken leadership regards the facility programs as experimental and developing. They regard the community service array as developing too. The major local industry, the steel mill, works twenty-four hours a day, and the group care facilities cannot meet the needs of parents working at "awkward" hours. In fact, some single mothers prefer such hours because of the bonus pay. Parents who work from 6:30 P.M. to 6:30 A.M. have no group care resource. Sandviken prefers family day care (accommodating children in private homes) in such cases—and for all children under two. Yet, there is discomfort with the family day-care programs here, as elsewhere in Sweden. A few of the homes are excellent, but some obviously are not. As elsewhere, screening of applicants for these day-care jobs deals only with the apartments' adequacy and with the absence of pathology. There is little ongoing inspection or consultation. Almost a third of the family day-care mothers have completed a voluntary ninety-hour course run by the municipality (even though there is no financial advantage in doing so). The family day-care job involves pressure (up to five children may be cared for in one home and may not be left), and there is no one with whom to share the responsibility. Nonetheless, some parents prefer these more informal, personal, close arrangements for their children, even though waiting-list data suggest that a larger number favor day nurseries. The professionals and political leaders emphasize the advantages of group care. At the central government level, in particular, family day care is written off as a long-term resource. Family day-care growth is not expected during the next several years despite the anticipated expansion of preschool programs. The central government subsidy pattern tends to make family care more expensive for the commune.

In the nearby town of Gavle, which shares the regional airport with Sandviken, we were told that the working-class and student clients prefer the center care arrangements. Nonetheless, 350 children are placed in family day care—licensed—with 320 women, many of whom have their own children. The fee for this care, per child, is the equivalent of one quarter of a modest weekly salary. The selection screening is modest, there is no training, and the central staff lacks time for real guidance. The placements are nonetheless very stable, even though other towns are said to have high turnover in family day care. (Since the staff turnover in the group facilities is almost everywhere high during the rapid expansion, family day care does not suffer the usual relative disadvantage in this regard in many parts of Sweden.)

Gavle offers further insights. First, Gavle has built in a working-class area an expensive, attractive day-nursery facility—such as is seen in most new towns in Sweden—in the midst of a housing cluster of high-rise and middle-level white brick. Again, the argument is "good, long-term economy."

When we walked into the rather large facility (two infant groups, two sibling groups, one two-year group, one play school for six year olds), there was remarkable "disorder." By the end of the day, nothing was on its shelf, in its cabinet, in its corner. But staff members were relaxed. As children left, the staff put everything in its place for the next day. This fits a child-care philosophy which holds that children should be left to deal freely with materials and equipment if they are to learn and grow. Such freedom would be unheard of in child-care programs of a dozen countries we have seen, even those far to the left of Sweden politically.

When we asked the staff in this facility (The Hilly Garden) what they would do if they had a disturbed child, they indicated that there had been no problems thus far. A little exploration revealed that there have been three brain-damaged children needing extra support; the medical authorities have been called upon for that, but a referral takes a long time. A boy needing psychological help has been sustained because in effect there is none in this area. A child with adjustment problems could be referred to a small day nursery—and we saw one which had only fifteen children—to provide a more intimate atmosphere. There is good cooperation with the well-baby clinic: the clinic will call if a child due for a checkup does not come in, and the day nursery staff can call if they feel that a child needs attention. (In this area there is routine health screening at the age of four, a policy being debated nationally as perhaps not justifiable in the light of the costs and medical shortage. The age-four examination checks sight, hearing, and balance and seeks problems or defects not obvious in younger children.)

In short, although nothing is ideal, these programs do work relatively well in the context of Sweden's excellent provision for child-health services.

Some of the Context

The Sandviken and Gavle programs reflect national leadership and subsidization. Local government, which has the major operating role for services in Sweden, raises considerable funds through income taxes. Programs such as the preschool efforts are therefore dependent on local response to national initiative and considerable local administrative and financial commitment.

Central government contributes lump sums on a matching basis to localities for the costs of constructing child center facilities. It also contributes on a per-child basis to operating costs. In 1973, for example, while doubling the per-place construction subsidy to about $2,400, the government maintained the operating contribution of about $1,000 per year per preschool child and $500 per year per school-age child (for before- or after-school care).[3] Central government also reimburses about 35 percent of expenditures for family day-care mothers. The rest of the operating costs are met by locality and parent fees. The approximate overall distribution is 35 percent from central government, 50 percent from local government, and 15 percent from parents. (Local government and parents pay far smaller shares of costs for all but proprietary day care and preschool in the United States).

Most Swedish child-center programs are run by municipal authorities through child-welfare authorities or (in far fewer instances) educational or other authorities. Here, as in other countries, the debate continues as to whether these programs should be part of education or of social-welfare programs. There is agreement that they should be non-stigmatic, universal social services. The dominant view also favors the

3. Here, as throughout the volume, we have converted to U.S. dollar equivalents on the basis of average exchange rates at the time of writing. It was a period of some fluctuation in the dollar in European exchanges. Our U.S. totals are rounded. Readers will recognize that actual costs and fees have increased during the 1975 inflation; however, the relationships and trends are unchanged.

social welfare administrative designation. Some programs are county or privately run. There are practically no industrial programs in Sweden. Standard-setting and inspection is by the National Board of Health and Welfare and the local county administration.

Expansion has been rapid and considerable since the adoption in the 1960s of a government policy to stress all-day care, to see all facilities as combining child-development and educational approaches, and to unify administration of child centers and family day care. In 1950 there were only 9,321 places in day nurseries and 18,326 in play schools (now called part-time groups), all in 713 centers. Family day care was dominant. Table 1 shows the expansion of public services to families with children since 1960; it should be recalled that elementary school begins at the age of seven. In addition, in 1972 there were some 10,000 free-time center places for school-age children over seven needing care before and after school hours, and the total was 13,500 in 1973. Projections from local plans to 1977 show a stabilization of the family day-care figure and considerable growth in day nurseries (over 83,000), in part-time groups (139,000 children), and in free-time centers (over 27,000).

TABLE 1
EXPANSION OF PUBLIC SERVICES TO FAMILIES WITH CHILDREN SINCE 1960

Year	Day nurseries (no. of places)	Family day care (no. of children)	Part-time groups (no. of children)
1960	10,300	4,000	38,400
1965	11,900	8,000	52,100
1970	33,000	32,000	86,000
1971	41,000	41,500	91,000
1972	46,400	43,500	96,000
1973*	54,600	44,500	101,000
1974*	62,800	51,000	108,000

*Estimated figure.

The coverage rate is best conveyed by noting that, in 1972, 25 percent of all 800,000 preschool children in the country were enrolled in either part-day or all-day preschool facilities or in family day care.[4] The data also suggest that in 1972 a very large proportion of day

4. Of course coverage is uneven: Stockholm meets half its needs, in this sense, while some areas meet insignificant percentages.

nursery space was occupied by children whose parents both worked full time or part time (if there were two parents) or were single parents who worked. There are no comparable data for part-day programs or for family day care. All-day care was available to 12 percent of all children born 1966–72; part-day care covered another 13 percent. Also, 35.5 percent of families with children in all-day preschool centers were single parents. Whether coverage is "adequate" depends on the evaluation of the part-time group care and the family day-care places. The age coverage of the system in 1973 can be seen in Table 2.

TABLE 2

PERCENTAGE OF CHILDREN IN VARIOUS AGE-COHORTS SERVED BY SWEDISH CHILD-CARE FACILITIES

Age cohort (in years)	Day nurseries	Part-time groups	Family day care
Five	8.7	14.3	6.1
Four	8.8	2.6	6.3
Three	8.4	0.5	5.4
Two	7.4	0.0	4.9
One	5.3		4.5
Less than one	2.5		4.4

Preschool leadership in Sweden feels that considerable expansion of all-day resources is still needed. Legislation passed in 1973 guarantees places to all six year olds by 1975 and projects expansion downward; the needs of all disadvantaged, deprived, and handicapped children are to be met almost immediately.

After long debate and the much-publicized work of the influential 1968 Commission on Child Centres, whose recommendations are still guiding legislative enactments and central administration practice, Swedish authorities have in recent years stressed the joining of both child-developmental and educational objectives in these programs. They reject the notion that programs must be custodial *or* educational *or* oriented largely toward a child's emotional development and socialization. They also reject the notion that there is a contradiction between meeting the needs of parents (for whom the mother's work is a matter of economic and personal importance) and those of the children. While affirming the primacy of the home, in short, Swedish officials see validity in and need for community provision. Thus, in the words of the Commission on Child Centres:

The responsibility for the upbringing, supervision, and care of children rests chiefly with the home. The community has, however, to a great extent undertaken a responsibility within this field, among other ways through the provision of child centres by local authorities. Changes in the family structure and living conditions have brought a greatly increased demand for public measures to assist parents with the care of their children. In increasing numbers of families both parents go out to work. For unmarried and divorced parents organized child care is a condition for their ability to support the family by paid work. Child centres also fulfill an important educational function in teaching children group activities under pedagogic guidance.

The "pedagogic" discussions are dominated by Swedish applications of the child-development concepts of Erik H. Erikson, Piaget, and some psychoanalytic thinkers. The leadership stresses offering experiences which promote ego development, concept formulation, and communication skills. Close cooperation with parents is seen as essential, as is a proper physical setting for the preschool program and appropriate organizational models. The emphasis is on personality development, not on preempting the elementary schools' responsibility for teaching reading, writing, and arithmetic. The major approaches involve giving a child enough inner security to permit him extensive explorations in interpersonal contacts and use of environments and materials. The adults guide the children through "a continuous dialogue . . . on both an inward and outward level, with mutual giving and taking in respect to feelings, experiences, and knowledge. . . . Respect for the child as an active individual . . . is a necessary condition."

The staffing ratios must be high to implement such an approach, and staff training becomes essential. At present, staffs meet the numerical-size requirements, but are often insufficiently trained by Swedish criteria. Thus, the National Board of Health and Welfare recommends: (1) at least two qualified preschool teachers per preschool all-day unit and an overall ratio of one staff person for five children aged two and a half to seven (not including staff for food service) and one staff person for four children under two and a half; (2) at least one qualified teacher per forty children in the part-day programs (two groups of twenty, each for three hours) for five and six year olds, and one teacher per thirty children (two groups of fifteen) for four and five year olds; (3) the employment of child nurses to work with very young children while there is a shortage of qualified teachers; (4) a director for each center; and (5) reserving a quota of jobs for males if they can be recruited and trained.

Preschool in Örebro

We can get some insights into the problems of implementing such goals if we look at the experience of Örebro, a middle-sized Swedish town of 115,000 whose age distribution approximates that of the country as a whole.[5] Örebro is an industrial town, two-and-a-half hours from Stockholm by train, in the center of the country. Declining shoe and clothing industries have been replaced by other, diverse, manufacturing activities (foodstuffs, building materials, electrical supplies, paper). There is still significant agriculture, employing almost 8 percent of the workers. The communal government includes the town, five rural districts, and a parish. The countryside is pleasant. The city itself has a lovely lake at its center, and residential expansion features "small towns within the town," each with the major amenities. As is generally the case in new Swedish areas, multiple dwellings rather than detached houses are featured. There is an emphasis on color, design, harmony of elements, amenity, in providing facilities for all social classes. Indeed, a foreigner cannot easily tell whether a housing unit will most probably serve upper-middle-class professionals, Yugoslav or Finnish immigrants, or typical skilled Swedish workers—or in what combinations.

One such new area of 5,500 people is called Brickebacken, two-and-a-half miles from the Örebro center, settled only since 1970. Most of the buildings are of the two-story garden type, quite long. They are well placed in relation to land contours. Community facilities share a service center (well-serviced with a large parking lot), with bank, post office, restaurant, the usual shopping resources. Thus, in one small area there are a medical center and dental service, a school, a restaurant-pub (which doubles as the school cafeteria), a nursery school, the well-baby clinic, a library (shared by town and school), a church, a sports center with pool and sauna (also shared), and game and hobby rooms (which also serve as school shops) for various community uses. All these facilities are linked by protected, covered galleries. Colors are used with imagination and daring: rusts, oranges, red brick, greens. The environment is pleasant and the internal pedestrian "traffic" mingles school children with the aged, nursery groups, and parents out on shopping errands.

We visited the Hopprepet (The Jumping Rope), a play school and

---

5. The distribution is as follows: ages 0–6 (preschool), 10 percent of the population; ages 7–17 (school age), 13 percent; ages 18–66 (working age), 64 percent; and ages 67 and over ("pensionable"), 13 percent.

day nursery on the Björkrisvagen (Birch Twig Road) in front of the Brickebacken center. It is one of two such schools, at opposite ends of this new town, and is housed in a pleasant, low, prefabricated redwood building, surrounded by a spacious playground.

The facility is essentially a corridor with four "apartments" for the children. On the right side are club rooms, staff rooms, and common facilities such as kitchen and sitting room. One "apartment" is actually a rather elaborate club-room arrangement manned by a church group and available to school-age youths in the afternoons. Any of the large rooms may be used by the center groups during the day.

We visited the day-care center first.[6] There are three groups, each with fifteen children and two staff members—an "early childhood teacher" and somebody who has either nursing background or no special training. The children look healthy, well developed, well dressed. They come from an essentially white-collar population. Many of the parents are students and others work in white-collar jobs. The place is well equipped, with sophisticated, modern play equipment, much of it ingenious. The colors are attractive.

This center has shifted from the traditional age segregation to the recommended "sibling groups" of children aged three to seven. Adding children from a waiting list as spaces become available is simple and assures efficient space utilization and what the leadership considers a sound milieu for optimum development. The sibling groups have occasional afternoon visits from school-age children. Eighteen children in the seven-to-ten age group are registered here for daily attendance. According to the locally responsible official, "we find it important to let the school child, who has been placed previously in the day nursery, come back to the same center if he wishes in order to feel secure and at home during the early school years." Most of the children arrive at 7:00 or 7:30 A.M. and are picked up between 5:00 and 6:00 P.M., but some stay until 6:30, when the center closes.

The "apartment" for each group of fifteen children has a room which can be used for eating and a variety of quiet play, as well as a large room for very active play where mattresses can also be spread out for sleeping. There is a small room for isolation and withdrawal for children who become ill during the day or want to be alone, and there is also appropriate room space for cooking and equipment. Although the play-

6. "Day-care center" seems like the most natural term for use by us here to describe a facility offering all-day or part-day care. Of course this is a day nursery and part-time group (play school) within a joint center, in the Swedish sense.

ground cannot boast of the hilly, tree-studded terrain that we saw used to such advantage elsewhere, it contains sand, ladders, and every imaginable kind of equipment.

We remained for a while to watch the children have their afternoon snack: sandwiches with cheese, sausage, cold meat, or some other protein, plus raw vegetables and a glass of juice, tea, or cocoa. The day nursery follows about the same daily schedule as do most child centers in Sweden: breakfast at about 8:00, lunch at 12:00, a nap after lunch, a snack about 4:00.

None of the Örebro child centers cook the main courses for meals, but rather serve so-called "KG-food"—industry-prepared food deep frozen in portions of six—which is warmed in the day-nursery kitchens. Even though the children can take as much as they want, this system is less expensive than cooking in each center. Moreover, since the children may help the cook in preparing vegetables, salads, and sandwiches, each school can manage with only one cook.

Americans ask regularly about staff and administration contact with the parents. The local inspector is frank: "We have the traditional parent meetings and also a parent association. But we do not really have close cooperation. Many of the parents are young students. And staff is young and often insecure. There is heavy staff turnover—the usual problem in a 'female' profession with many young women getting married and having their own children. Sometimes I have a feeling that parents just deposit their children. Both parts, young parents and young staff, seem afraid of each other."

This phenomenon is not unusual for Sweden. We heard of it in other day nurseries, but less frequently where the staff was mature and stable. Very active parent participation, as in cooperative American nursery schools, some day-care centers, and many Head Start programs, is unusual. Swedish parents seem to have little to say about the organization and "routine" of the day nursery. At most they may create an association of parents of the day nurseries or preschools in the township. They concern themselves with things like the height of fences or the kind of equipment needed. They want to be consulted about major steps, such as new fees or new programs, but they are not pushing for management influence or "community control." There is trust here in the child-care "experts." Although the staff do discuss a child with his parents and take his family background into consideration in working with him, both parents and staff seem quite shy about all this and not a great deal comes of it. In general the staff seem undereducated and inexperienced in this realm, a major deficiency. We also learned, in a series of discussions, that there are deviant and troubled children in centers and that staff are often not equipped to help them; moreover, some localities have a shortage of social and psychological services. The social-service program in Örebro is oriented largely toward income-maintenance issues and has no child-welfare field staff to assume this kind of task.

A doctor visits each center for checkups and consultation every week. He is assisted by two qualified nurses, one of them full-time. The center also cooperates closely with the well-baby clinic in the Bricke-backen center. Special attention is paid to infants. If they catch infections too frequently and do not thrive, they may be transferred to family day-care homes. Since it is in close contact with local families, the well-baby clinic often helps to locate homes for this purpose.

We briefly visited the infants and toddlers in the separate wing, which is five minutes' walking distance from the older children's center. Here, a staff of three "child nurses" care for eleven children ranging in age from six months to two years. The inventive room decoration offers stimulation for small children. Big light balloons in different sizes and colors hang on strings from the ceiling, so that babies lying on mattresses or crawling on the floor can easily reach and play with them. A wall mirror which extends to the floor lets babies take a full-size look at themselves. There are tubs for water, sand play, and finger painting. All pictures—some of them paintings made by the older children for the small ones—are placed low so that the babies can look at them at their own eye level. And so are the shelves, which are full of attractive play materials and musical instruments. Much of the equipment has been made by the staff, obviously with love and ingenuity, and the children can easily choose what to play with. The most original thing in the room is a scarlet, inflated, undulating plastic "floor," where the children can crawl "uphill and down" and rest comfortably when tired. (This type of mattress is especially useful for children with motor handicaps, according to the nurse.) The toddlers in the room seemed very secure. They gave their visitors some quick scrutinizing looks, then continued playing around in the room and patting their nurse.

The children arrive at 7:30 or 8:00 A.M. During our visit, most were picked up by 3:00 or 4:00 P.M., although two were still present at 5:30. The locally responsible official agreed, as did most of the personnel in a number of local programs with whom we discussed the matter, that the days are far too long for the children. By the time they go home, they are over-tired, even though they take long naps, out of doors whenever possible, in their own carriages or on mattresses and cots supplied by the center. The child-care workers are essentially para-professionals; several told us that when they have their own children, they will leave this work for a while. They do not want their infants in all-day care because they regard the day as too long and impersonal for a very small child despite the high staff-to-child ratios. Most would prefer some kind of program offering both personal-intimate care and the group experience. Despite this, there has not been any strong support for family day care on the central government level. The ideology of the leadership in Sweden is in favor of group facilities: "It is better for a child's development." However, we found some local officials who favor a mixed system. Some would accept a "clustered" arrangement in which children spent half the day in an essentially family day-care facility and half the day in group programs.

Örebro has slowed expansion of its centers in the face of high costs and the local election defeat of the long-dominant party. Parents here, as everywhere in Sweden, pay for the service in accordance with a sliding scale tied to income level. The national range which applies generally is from about $.69 to $5.75 per child per day. At the time of our visit, the daily operating cost was at least double the maximum fee. In a sense, then, it is public policy to subsidize low-paying industry by freeing mothers to work, and even to subsidize relatively privileged parents. Of course, scarce spaces are assigned according to socially assessed need (families where both parents work, single-parent families, low-income families, families in which the parent or child requires personal help, etc.). In Örebro, as elsewhere, continued growth of the program is expected. The tradition of providing for social equipment (a French term) in housing developments, especially day-care centers, schools, health facilities, and resources for the aged, seems strongly anchored.

Day Care in Göteborg

Göteborg (Gothenburg), a west coast Swedish city founded in the thirteenth century, is one of the country's main urban centers. Its economy is based on commerce, shipbuilding, and manufacturing. Its docks and riverfront industry remind one of many major ports in Europe or the United States. The city itself contains over 450,000 people, but the larger metropolitan area has a population of 700,000.

Although the city's social policy is relatively conservative by Swedish standards, like most Swedish municipalities Göteborg has a "social administration" or "public welfare" department administering local "centers." The central office has five major units: social assistance (administering the district centers), care of children and youth, care of old people, labor welfare, and leisure time centers. One bureau in the "children and youth" unit provides city-wide leadership for the "pre-school" and "family day home" undertakings, but there is also much decentralization to local leadership based in the six district centers. At the time of our visit, the day-care program encompassed over three hundred "preschools" and seven hundred family day homes and was growing almost monthly. To serve the approximately 36,000 children under seven, Göteborg has the following resources: 120 day nurseries, capable of providing all-day care for 4,000 children aged six months to seven years; 65 free-time centers, providing before- and after-school care for up to eleven hundred seven to twelve year olds; 150 play schools (three hours daily for each of two groups or one group daily for four or five hours), with space for 6,000 children, mostly five and six year olds; and 700 family day-care homes, accommodating up to 1,300 children aged six months to twelve years, but mostly of preschool ages. To this should be added 170,000 hours of care of sick children by a part-time staff of 1,000 women who cover for working parents who cannot stay home when their children fall ill. The fee paid by these parents is the same as the day-care fee.

Our first visit was to a small play school, in a converted red farm-house behind the old-age center. The previous teacher had created a center with special character: she had a large collection of animals, and the children also worked on growing fruits and vegetables. Under the present teacher, the school remains an informal place, attractive and pleasant, with a relaxed atmosphere. Since the building is small, there are only fifteen children, all of whom live nearby. There is no industrial day care here since the town does not believe it is sound for children to travel with their parents to work. They would not forbid it, but they will not subsidize it.

Our next visit was to a larger facility in Önnered, a middle-class area of Göteborg. The typical day-nursery or preschool program here has three groups: one for about ten children from eighteen months to three years old, usually staffed by two "nurses"; one group for about fifteen three to five year olds, staffed by two preschool teachers; and one group of about eighteen five to seven year olds, also staffed by two preschool teachers. (In short, the "sibling-group" reform has not yet been accepted in Göteborg.) In addition, the centers often provide after-school care for a group of about fifteen seven to twelve year olds or, less often, before-school care for children who go to school after their mothers go to work. Two teachers work with this "free-time" program.

The city-wide program director is not enthusiastic about group programs for the children under two. While he appreciates the opposing views among child-care experts and advocates of full equality of women, he is not convinced that such programs are good for the children developmentally; moreover, infections spread easily, and staff turnover is high. Indeed, he is not over-eager to encourage the entrance of children under three. However, he recognizes that some infant group programs are needed in view of labor-market trends and the needs of young parents who are students, and he tries to make them sound. They are staffed by nurses.

A special feature here at Önnered is its male "nurse." A small number of men are now being attracted to day-care work and are valued for their contribution to the center environment—and for their ability to help with heavy lifting and moving. A space quota in training programs is gradually increasing male representation. Some of the recruits are conscientious objectors for whom this is an acceptable substitute for military service.

The typical Göteborg day nursery is open from 6:30 A.M. to 6:30 P.M., Monday to Friday. Sometimes there are Saturday hours. In addition to the staff members mentioned above, it has a director, one or more cooks, and cleaning help. The annual cost to the local community for all-day care is over $2,000 for older children and $2,400 for younger children. Even the top fees do not cover half the operating costs, not to mention capital costs and overall administration expenses.[7]

The Göteborg programs, like most of the Swedish programs we visited, have a child-centered permissive climate and an extremely attentive, if very young, staff. These features seemed to a visitor more important than whether programs have adopted "sibling grouping" or retained age groupings, or whether they have followed literally the Reform Commission's proposals for the physical facility—a central, shared, activity space and "home room."

In the typical center, here, each group has two large rooms for quiet and active play, naps (for those who need them), eating. There are also child-sized washroom and toilet facilities and individual bins and clothes-hanging closets or hooks for personal possessions. Almost everywhere,

---

7. Plans are under discussion to institute a uniform monthly fee, between the extremes of the current scale, payable whether or not a child attends each day.

the rooms are big, light, and gaily colored, with lots of solid play material of good quality. Big wooden toys are a Swedish specialty. Here, the food is cooked in the kitchen, which the groups share in common. Children are served breakfast, lunch, and an afternoon snack. But each section—except for the toddlers'—also has a miniature, children's-size kitchen with real ovens to let the children experiment with cooking, baking, and washing up. All the rooms open directly onto the large outdoor playground, where the smallest children have a fenced-in area to themselves. Nearest the doors are robust wooden wind-, snow-, and rain-sheltered verandas, where children play with sand, clay, and finger painting, when the weather permits. A visitor notes the obvious pleasure of the healthy-looking toddlers in their veranda play.

As we entered the Önnered afterschool group, two staff members were helping two children arrange a photograph album. Another was sewing curtains. The mix of seven to thirteen year olds seems to work well. Here, as elsewhere on our visits, the staff is extremely young and attractive. We were impressed with the intelligence of all staff members as they talked about their responsibilities. Just as the facilities are new and shiny, the teachers are young, since the development is rapid and new. It will be a long time before those communities where day-care expansion has been rapid have the mature and experienced staffs found in the industrial towns and cities with older programs.

In this particular center in Önnered, staff are backed by a "pedagogical consultant" and try to intervene if children have school problems or the parents appear troubled. They may undertake school or home visits. A similar pattern is being encouraged nationally but is as yet rare.

The second wing of this play school has a group of twelve normal children and four hard-of-hearing children. For the latter there is a specially equipped laboratory with a variety of devices and equipment, and they receive help from a play-school teacher who has had supplementary training for several years. Outside, beyond the high rise, we noticed a rather informal wooden clubhouse for other children and a small shack run by the park department. A bit further down the road is a scout house.

Play-school centers in Göteborg typically charge the parents from $2.60 to $11.00 monthly, and cost $400 per child per year, apart from capital costs. One teacher usually staffs two groups a day, 8:30–11:30 A.M. and 12:30–5:30 P.M., and groups typically consist of twenty children aged five and six. The service is open only nine months a year, Monday through Friday, and is thus a popular place to work. (There are a few such facilities for three-and-a-half to four year olds, offering three-hour programs, and these limit groups to fifteen children.)

In one particularly attractive facility, an elementary school and a play school share a gym and indoor play spaces. One wing has four "home rooms" for seven- and eight-year-old primary school classes, in groups of twenty-five. The opposite wing offers rooms for four play-school groups of twenty children.

Although Sweden has done much to assure a basic "social minimum" to all—and has a larger proportion of its population living in housing built since World War II than any country in the world—not all its people live in colorful new town areas or attend brand new centers and schools. Thus, Göteborg has what it considers to be an old, deteriorated inner-city area. One of the worst spots is in the Haga district. Some of the blocks, formerly occupied by typically poor families, with fifty- and sixty-year-old buildings, are now being restored and freshly painted. A group of apartments has been converted into a day nursery, with enough space for the usual three groups. There is also a unit for after-school youth. But here too, in this more traditional building, one flight up, with its mixture of old and new furniture and with its quite senior staff, we find that the program quality and character can be protected. Despite municipal prerogatives, there is great similarity—albeit attractive similarity—in all these programs: the same three groups, the same age groupings, and essentially the same functions performed, even though the kinds of equipment and details of the approaches may vary from place to place. The children are generally healthy-looking and relaxed, even though occasionally one notes a withdrawn, disturbed, retarded, or handicapped child who has deliberately been integrated into the regular groups as part of child-care policy.

The young ones here, too, often seem very tired late in the day.[8] We saw many little children who arrived at 6:30 or 7:00 in the morning and were not picked up until 4:00 or 5:00. Similarly, we noted that in the after-school programs for the seven to thirteen year olds, the search for privacy and quiet is not always successful if the facility is not extremely well designed and run. These problems must be considered even by day-care enthusiasts.

But free-time centers for the hours before and after school (essential if parents work and valuable in any case) are widely approved, even

8. Of course, even at home very young children get tired by the end of the day. Several groups in Sweden are now actively advocating a six-hour work day for both men and women to permit more parental participation in child care, better family life generally, and—incidentally—a shorter nursery day.

though capacities are still limited. We visited one such place which is not attached to a preschool. The entire facility is devoted to before- and after-school care. Imagine a row of high-rise buildings in a residential area built in the 1940s and 1950s, in which the lower floor was converted into schoolrooms at the time of the original construction. As additional high rises grew in the area, a special schoolhouse had to be built. This low-income community did something interesting. It created a schoolhouse in which each classroom is in effect a yellow brick rectangle, with internal protected play space. With the space vacated in the lower floors of the high rise, it was possible to organize a free-time school. There are thirty children, ages seven to thirteen, in two groups. Thirty percent come before school since their parents go to work before school opens or work late shifts. The rest come after school and stay until the closing at 6:30. The center's philosophy is persuasive. They feel that since the children have had exciting days and really need a homelike atmosphere, they should be able to choose between group activity and privacy. So there are places for escape; one of the most interesting is a double-story cabinlike compartment with stairs at one side, a simple ladder built by the staff along the wall, and berths behind the "board" wall. For groups, there are craft and reading rooms and tables for homework, as well as the usual space for play and climbing and an outdoor area.

Where children want "action," the setup can be exemplary. One of the gayest, most colorful, and permissive places for children we saw in Sweden was also in the Haga district in Göteborg, in a former public bath. The center shares the old building with some light industry. One enters a basement with low vaults, rearranged as a play "paradise" for schoolchildren's leisure time. The children are welcome to come and go as they wish. The place was built up with the help of the children and their parents. It is equipped as an indoor adventure playground with slides and ladders from the upper stories and all sorts of odd material for "creative work." It is a strange mixture of the surreal, the rough, the primitive. The place is headed by an energetic young woman, assigned as an "activator" ("group leader" in the United States) and with special training in early childhood education, handicrafts, and art. She is permissive but not careless.

Day Care in Huddinge

The recommendations of the Commission on Child Centres did not answer all questions, but they generated the kind of ferment that gives rise to further innovation. We may illustrate with an overview of the situation in Huddinge, a relatively short distance from central Stockholm.[9] A large new town is firmly anchored in the area; the brightly colored, multiple dwellings are well placed in the lovely landscape; and there is an effort to preserve beauty and create amenity. The scale is kept human.

First we visited several "ordinary" preschool centers, and then a play school which also has a play-advice program in the afternoon (since rescheduled to the morning). The first facility we visited, here classified as a family day nursery, is simple, serving only fifteen children. Five of them attend for part of the day, and the other ten are there all day long. The staff consists of two full-time and three part-time teachers. They do their own cooking. In contrast to some other places we saw, the wooden building is modest and everything is on a smaller scale and in a lower key. The room for sleeping is warm and quiet, and children sleep on mattresses on the floor, an arrangement deliberately chosen in preference to cots because it permits flexibility and initiative.

The next facility is larger. Like others we visited it is built in a horseshoe arrangement. The main big playroom has windows on both sides and has an outdoor feeling. In fact, it is connected with the playground. The other rooms are in the closed wings.

Then we visited Nyponet (The Hyphen), which utilizes ground-floor space in a residential dwelling. Nyponet has an ordinary half-day playschool program for twenty children six years old and also an "open play school" for children who are accompanied by parents and who range in age from eight down. The program serves families in which a parent is at home for at least a half-day. This also is a special experimental program, guided by a very young-looking twenty-eight-year old who tackles her work creatively, devotes herself to it completely, and clearly inspires confidence in parents older than herself. The experimental task, funded nationally at the time of the visit, but now on the local budget, is to welcome—whenever they wish to come—parents who accompany their children and to increase their confidence and competence in playing with their children.

The facility has a big entry hall, a small director's office, and two big, light rooms full of play material for active and more quiet play. There is the usual miniature kitchen and a washroom.

The experimental "open play school" functions three mornings weekly, nine months of the year. The mothers usually come with two to

9. For more detail about Huddinge, see Chapter 7.

four year olds but sometimes bring infants. At the time of our visit the daily average was ten mothers but there were thirty-five on peak days. The visits may be brief or may last three hours.

The mothers are obviously enthusiastic. Mrs. A., who came with her two-and-a-half-year-old son and three-month-old daughter, praised the center highly: "I find the place marvelous. We began to come here in January after I found a municipal advertisement about the arrangement in our local newspaper. The best thing about it is that you can stay here with the child. Tommy does not want to leave me yet. I have tried to have him at the local day nursery while I was at work. He does not seem mature enough for it; he just kept crying all the time. Here, on the other hand, he plays happily with the other children—as long as I stay here." Her baby lay on a mattress and looked at the children around her. Now and then someone came up to hug her and play with her and she chuckled happily. "It is nice for me to meet and get to know other mothers here. I wish there had been such a place when Tommy was small, too. I was very isolated then and did not dare to talk to unknown neighbors. When you are a newcomer in a block like this you do not dare to start talking to people. They seem to think you are funny if you do. . . . It is not like in a small town. But here I dare to open up a conversation. Everything is so much easier in a place like this, and you do not have to be afraid that the children will spoil something, like in the shops or at the grocer's. It is the only place to go with the children, except for the outdoor playground. It is too much trouble to try to go to 'town' (Stockholm) in the subway with a baby carriage and a toddler like Tommy."

Mrs. H., who brought her five-year-old daughter and five-month-old son, agreed: "It is good for Elena to get some playmates. Most other children of her age go to the day nursery. She needs a place like this. She gets restless going around alone with me and Tomas in the flat all day. It suits us perfectly to come here early in the morning when they open up at 9:00, to spend three hours here and get back home for lunch. Elena would like to come here every morning, though. Tomas seems to profit, too, from seeing other children. He seems so amused and is much more tired the days we have been here. He must have taken in a lot, I guess."

Mrs. M. H. had come with her three-and-a-half-year-old granddaughter: "I have been looking for a place like this for a year. The girl is so bright and curious. But to whatever program I have taken her before, for instance to a skating school, they just told me: 'She is too small to begin yet. Come back when she is four years old.' And for myself it is such a pleasure to come and see all these children playing so interestedly with all the fine material here."

The program seems aimed at reassuring the mother, showing her how other people deal with the children and how equipment is used. The children are helped in learning to share and participate. There is some cooperation with a well-baby clinic since one nurse makes referrals, and there is also cooperation with a mental-health center with one social worker. The degree of participation seems to suggest that the center meets a need. Two other facilities participating in the experiment use the morning periods in part-time group centers for the same purpose, and there is one Saturday center which serves over fifty people in one day.

Half of all the mothers who come are family day-care mothers who want to learn more about caring for children by observing the nursery-school teachers. When programs are open on Saturday, a significant number of fathers come. Thus, there are two different kinds of needs being served in the "open play school": The young, inexperienced, isolated mothers get the sort of reassurance that comes from watching others take care of children and from playing with their children in an environment with others. The family day-care mothers come to learn about equipment and program and how trained teachers and nurses cope with children. They also come to end their own isolation and expose their charges to a group situation.

The visiting parents and family day-care mothers make good use of the bookshelf of child-rearing and child-play materials. Everything—books, pamphlets, toys—is well used but nothing disappears. Special course recruiting also takes place at the six experimental centers. The response has been so positive that the municipality will take over when the experimental funding ends. Nyponet is seen as a relatively effective preventive service.

The Context

We have been describing day-care programs here as independent entities, but Swedish proponents insist that they are understood and accepted only as part of an overall social policy. Day care works in Sweden partly because it is embedded in a broader social commitment. It is accepted as "natural," defined as an appropriate public responsibility, in a society which does not question the priority assigned to whatever it takes to assure healthy physical growth and wholesome social and emotional development for all children. The Swedes conduct no tight, narrow cost-benefit calculations. The measures adopted include: (1) a basic cash children's allowance paid to all families with children; (2) paid parent leave for seven months after a child's birth; (3) regular free health check-ups for all children at well-baby clinics, and basic health coverage for all; (4) free hot school lunches for all children through secondary school; (5) housing subsidies for many, including families with several children. In effect, this is what it takes to maximize results of investment in any child-care program. To leave some of these measures out is to create competition among the parts which should constitute the whole.

Yet this is hardly the total picture. We were told by some of the leading Swedish day-care advocates that daytime care programs and complementary activities are justified by and must be understood in connection with even larger social goals: the achievement of equality for women and the consequent reconstruction of family life so that both men and women have "double" roles. The dominant note sounded in recent social-policy debate, the heart of domestic political discussion, is the desire to maximize parental sharing and individual options in work and daily life. A major political force has been assembled on behalf of preschool programs, explained by some as the result of the large-scale movement of women into the labor force and by others in terms of these more basic social commitments. In any case, it is assumed that society is obligated to provide for all children who need care and whose parents elect to use it. Child-care resources of high quality are seen as essential and the relation between fees and economic costs, between overall costs and societal economic reforms, is not probed in the public discussion.

In the economic slump of 1973, after an election in which taxpayers allegedly expressed displeasure at high tax rates, Swedish central authorities offered local communes higher reimbursement to construct facilities for preschool programs as a countercyclical job-creation measure, and continued their operating subsidies. During mid-1974, when inflation and other economic problems plagued industrialized countries, long-range planning for preschool expansion by local authorities was being mandated by the central leadership (even though guarantees were limited to six-year-olds).

None of this commitment and expansion ends debate, however. After all, there are significant shortages and waiting lists, local fund limitations which affect receipt of central government matching funds, and program questions. The following topics constantly recur in the Swedish press debate and political discussion: the rate of expansion, the age of entrance, group care versus family day care, program quality (including staffing qualifications and ratios), and parent-teacher cooperation.[10] Central leadership is highly oriented to equality goals and is dedicated to group care as better for children, despite the lack of conclusive research evidence. At the local level, opinions are more mixed and one encounters both parents and administrators who prefer family-care arrangements. Some believe that group situations are difficult for very young children, offer too little individualization, are tiring. While a recent, small, and perhaps not representative study showed that parental preference varies with the ages of the children involved and that family day care is popular for the one to three year olds (home care with relatives or nurses being preferred for the younger children, if parents cannot manage), other data offer a different perspective. Waiting lists are largely for scarce day-nursery spaces. Parents who have experienced center care for their children apparently prefer it. Thus authorities are concentrating planning on group facilities (which, in turn, affects preferences, one would assume). In fact, between 1966 and 1975, central government subsidized day nurseries but not part-time groups, a policy recently reversed—perhaps in response to the fact that this mode of care is often preferred and that as many as two-thirds of all employed women work only part time.

The sibling groupings, the permissive play-school atmosphere, the individualization, the imaginative buildings and equipment are exciting to visitors to Swedish programs, even though it is obvious that no model should be imported without modification, since each country, region, and community must develop its own culturally appropriate forms. The youth and turnover of staff are inevitable problems in a recently and rapidly expanded effort, and the issue of balance among personnel with different types of credentials requires attention and testing. Overall, however, these are normal and "good" problems.

Americans are surprised at the relatively low levels of parent-teacher contact and parent participation in Swedish programs. Obviously, participation is difficult for parents who work. Authorities also recognize that teachers are inexperienced in working with parents and shy about initiating it. An outside observer might add that, in a relatively homogeneous society like Sweden's, citizens have more confidence in hired

10. A new training arrangement, in the context of Sweden's very extensive adult education system, allows men and women to qualify as preschool teachers (early childhood education would be the U.S. term) by entering one-year courses on the basis of five years of other relevant experience or a university social science qualification.

officials and civil servants, and in a sophisticated urban society people often tend to trust experts and specialists. Thus the "community control" movement in day care and in Head Start, an American product of the antipoverty "war," is not manifest in Sweden. Nonetheless, American research and Swedish experience and educational philosophy agree that the positive impact of programs on children depends significantly on close parental participation in the daytime care experience. We will all need to consider how this is to be accomplished in a daily living pattern often involving labor-force participation by both parents. Some Swedish policy advocates see the solution in a six-hour work day.

With some exceptions, Sweden avoids connecting its child-care arrangements with the parents' work place. Early-morning travel is not easy for children whether in autos or by mass transit. Nor do parents like such a pattern; they prefer child-care arrangements that are small and close to home. Only if more attention is paid to proposals that living-working arrangements be rearranged to bring them into closer proximity for a variety of social purposes will "day care at work" become a major Swedish or American system.

An "American Connection"

In Sweden, elementary school begins at seven, so the Swedes are proud of assuring preschool places for all six year olds by 1975, at parental option. For children with special needs, local authorities are striving to assure coverage from four, while gradually expanding resources to meet all needs for all-day or half-day group care, as defined by parents who choose to work. While the coverage rates in Sweden in this sense are low as compared with such countries as France and Israel and are not high compared with the United States, what is unusual is the consciousness of policy, the commitment to quality, and the planning for the future. Nor has Sweden achieved its own quantitative goals as yet. In part this is because Sweden does not define family day care as part of the long-term goal, and in part it is because they seek group-center coverage for younger children than are included in most American programs.

The United States has not yet chosen its goal or resolved conflicting objectives for preschool programs. The debate fluctuates among three alternatives: a commitment to child-care arrangements so that "welfare mothers" may be trained and/or compelled to work; assurance of good care arrangements for children of mothers who do work but cannot command such care in the marketplace; and the espousal of universal availability of child care as a prerequisite to the maximization of choices for women and also to wholesome child development. Proponents of the first alternative tend to argue that deprived children will develop better both intellectually and in general social competence in group milieus. Indeed some would argue that the extrafamilial exposure for young, deprived children is more important than day-time care when mothers work.

United States coverage data are outdated, but it is believed that about one-tenth of preschool children of working mothers are in organized group care, and one-fifth in family day care. However, almost 45 percent of the three to five year olds attend a kindergarten or a nursery school. The size of the group in need remains a matter of definition and debate—a matter, in short of goal clarification. During the past several years, cost realities in quality programs and the recognition that cognitive and emotional-social gains achieved in Head Start and related programs, however impressive and valuable per se, are sustained only if there is "follow-through" have made all the above rationales subjects for debate.

As future policies are considered, American planners understand that most "welfare mothers," even if employed, would earn less than the operational costs of development-oriented day care for two children and are likely to contribute less by way of productivity than the full costs of service to even one child. And universal day care, a goal of women's liberationists and many others, has costs which at a given moment are in serious competition with health insurance or a major reform of housing or income maintenance—current alternative policy claimants. Nonetheless, no one doubts that, in the long run, labor-market participation by American women will expand for both economic and "equality" reasons, that many parents prefer group daytime care for their children for full or half-days, that some children, perhaps even a majority of three and four year olds, have problems and needs best served in preschool settings, and that provisions will need to increase steadily—even if the specific expansion rate during a given year may be debated.

It is interesting to Americans who see a fragmentation among private nursery schools, Head Start (for poor children), day care (for children of low-income working parents, welfare-trainee parents, and parents with problems in the household), and special preschool programs in the public schools, that Sweden sees all preschool programs and complementary activities as components of one overall strategy. Efforts in the United States to decategorize, to plan and administer comprehensively despite diversity of funding and eligibility, have had limited success—yet are obviously indispensable. Perhaps, unlike the Swedes, we may also want to see the strong parental support for family day care and similar nongroup arrangements reflected fully in national policy. The very small initiatives to integrate the two systems would seem worthy of more attention. Would it be possible to connect family day-care mothers to group settings so that they might have the benefit of exposure to teachers and continuing guidance, while the young children have some group experience yet avoid long days in group settings? What would be the problems, the rewards, the costs, the requirements?

It would take a full study to develop American policy,[11] but the Swedish overview is instructive: daytime care does best if proponents and administration have a sense of where they want to go. Planning is facilitated if health coverage, child allowances, housing subsidies, and school-lunch programs are already established. Physical facilities for preschool are attractive and accessible if provision becomes part of overall municipal planning and is integrated with construction of community housing and facilities generally. And this field offers room for imagination, creativity, and sound provision if one can provide resources, assure community commitment, assemble good personnel, and make the staff feel that what they are doing is important.

11. We are completing such a study. Clearly, kindergarten, nursery school, day care have overlapping functions and programs and must all be considered as plans are made.

3

School Meals

in England

VIGOROUSLY attacking plates filled with meat and cheese pizzas, "chips" (french fried potatoes), carrots, and peas, a group of sixteen year olds in Manchester described their school meals as a "best buy." Considering the shockingly high prices of food in Britain today, thirty cents for a hot meal consisting of meat or fish, vegetables, potatoes, and dessert (and seconds if desired) certainly is a bargain. More than two-thirds of the students in this comprehensive high school, located in a large industrial city, take advantage of it. Perhaps because 60 percent of this group receive free meals, there is no apparent stigma attached to it. A stringent policy is maintained regarding anonymity for children entitled to free meals; however, some children are remarkably open and unselfconscious about it. One child gaily announced, "I'm free! I'm free this week!" No one commented or noticed, although one teacher said that similar remarks were often made by the children.

At a similar school in a London ghetto community, the figures were the same, but the scene was different. In order to attract more students and increase the number eating school lunch, an experiment in dining— a "cash cafeteria"—was designed in 1972. Each student receives her thirty-cent ticket for a meal, and uses it to buy whatever she wants at the cafeteria, up to that amount. If she buys more, she must pay extra. In the one year since the experiment began, the number of girls taking school lunch has more than doubled. Once again, 60 percent receive these thirty-cent tickets free, but since all use the same tickets there is no visible distinction between "free" and "paid" lunches. Most important though, from the point of view of both school and community, is that as a result of this new program afternoon truancy from school has declined drastically.

In contrast, in a village school in the wealthiest county in England, all but four of the children enrolled at the school eat at school, and only one child receives a free lunch. His are the only "poor" parents in the area. None of the teachers, administrators, or other children in this school full of healthy, scrubbed, well-dressed youngsters knows who he is, because the head of the school insists that anonymity be rigorously maintained. For the middle- and upper-middle-class parents of these children, the subsidized meals are openly described as a good buy. In addition, eating at school saves the children an extra trip to and from home; and, perhaps best of all, the children say eating lunch at school is a great opportunity to talk with friends and teachers and still have time to play outside or in school for an hour before classes resume.

So for middle-class or poor children in suburban or inner-city ghetto schools, the school meals program in Britain is considered a great "asset." Subsidized by the government, it is a universal service, available to all, rich or poor. It is economical for those who pay and a valuable benefit for those who receive it free. School meals are nutritious and, for the most part, tasty. They provide an opportunity for socializing with friends and teachers. And finally, as a side benefit in certain schools, afternoon truancy has been reduced, eliminating the possible "community nuisance" occurring when teenagers are roaming the streets when they should be at school. In fact, it is not surprising that every day in England and Wales more than five million children between the ages of five and seventeen—more than two-thirds of the children enrolled in the equivalent of our public schools—eat the school meal. And both central and local agents are constantly searching for ways to increase this number.

Although school meals have been provided for some children since the beginning of the century, and service was expanded during the depression, it was during World War II that concern for providing meals for children on a mass scale really developed. Initial universal provision of school meals was established by the Education Act of 1944, amended subsequently in 1969. Currently, subsidized meals are required by law to be provided by every school in England and Wales to every child desiring them; and free meals are provided to poor children. In this sense, the British program is very much like ours. However, it is in the legal requirement for all schools to participate in the program, the nature of the subsidy (all cash, no commodity contributions), the attitude toward free-meal provision, the rate of utilization (or what the British term "take-up"), and the strong efforts on the part of the central and local governments to encourage students to take school meals, that this program varies substantially from that in the United States.

Policies and Program: Who Does What

Certain basic regulations and policies regarding school meals are defined nationally for all schools. These include:

1. *The charge for the meal.* Since September 1971, this has been twelve pence, or thirty cents.

2. *The nutritional content of the meal.* This is meticulously specified to include one-third of the essential daily nutritional requirements of a child and to constitute the "main meal of the day." Strong efforts are made to enforce these standards.

3. *Eligibility requirements for receiving free meals.* Families receiving the equivalent of public assistance, in addition to others meeting certain minimum-income standards, are entitled to receive free meals.

4. *Regulations regarding provision of meals on other than school days.* Depending on the demand, meals are to be available on weekends, holidays, summer vacations.

5. *Regulations regarding provision of meals other than the main midday one.* For example, breakfasts, teas, and other snacks may be made available.

Also, at the national level, the Department of Education and Science, the administrative agency responsible for the program, maintains a Catering Advisory Unit which advises the local governmental units on technical matters concerned with the preparation and service of school meals and reviews the conditions under which meals are eaten and the social possibilities linked with the planning of the school day.

Certain other decisions, in particular those related to implementation of the school meal program, are decentralized. These, which are the responsibility of the local education authorities, include:

1. *The style of meal service.* Schools may use "family style," cafeteria, or "cash cafeteria" arrangements.

2. *The style of meal preparation.* Schools may offer fresh, prepared daily, "containered," or prefrozen meals.

3. *The location of meal service.* A separate dining room or cafeteria may be used, or dual-purpose facilities such as a gym or assembly hall.

4. *The extent of choice.* Schools may limit themselves to one menu for all or offer two or more choices.

5. *The number of sittings.* One or two are possible.

6. *The composition of the menu.* Menus are decided on autonomously, by the school meals organizer or by the head cook at each school.

The net cost of school meals is met by direct payments from parents or the children, local rates or taxes, and the national government. The latter provides a general grant to the local authorities, part of which goes to meet expenditures on school meals. This amount is directly related to the number of meals served in each local government jurisdiction. All new schools are required by law to include construction of kitchen and dining facilities. This, too, is financed by the central government. At present, almost all schools have such facilities, although in some, meals still have to be "transported" or brought in.

At present, the average cost of a meal is about 65¢. Although some schools provide cafeteria service with a fairly wide selection of foods at additional cost, regardless of the style of service and range of choice, by law every school must provide a basic meal which can be purchased by the child for thirty cents. In 1972, 64 percent of the children attending schools in England and Wales were receiving school meals, and for 1973 the figure is estimated at close to 70 percent. The price of the meal was raised by about one-third in 1971 and the rate of utilization decreased from 68 percent in 1970 to the present 64 percent, but is rapidly returning to the earlier figure. Such a slump occurs each time the price of a meal is increased. A concomitant concern is that the neediest children are most likely to be hurt by the increase, since the income criteria for free meals still leaves some relatively low-income children paying for their lunches. Of the more than five million children receiving school meals, about 17 percent do not pay; however, the high, all-cash subsidy does ensure a relatively low-cost meal for all.

The School Meals Program in Action: Bayford

Hertfordshire, in the greenbelt area surrounding London, is inhabited largely by upper-middle-class professionals and executives, most of whom commute daily to work in London, and has the highest per-capita tax rate of any county in England. Its American counterpart might be Westchester County in New York State, Fairfield County in Connecticut, or Montgomery County in Maryland. Bayford village, the site of one school visited, is a semirural, suburban community located approximately twenty miles from London, less than one hour by train. The green hilly landscape is dominated by one-family houses and farms;

however, only a very small percentage of the children attending the school come from local farm families. The school serves an area of twenty-five square miles, but most children come from two small nearby villages. The children are an unusually homogeneous group although their parents' occupations range from college faculty, stockbrokers, and movie directors to skilled workers and small shopkeepers. Like those in similar communities in the United States, parents tend to be actively interested in their children's education and well-being. It is a commentary on how they view the program that more than 70 percent of the children in the county as a whole and 95 percent of the children in this village school take school meals. The proportion of those who receive free meals in the county generally is relatively low (20 percent); in this school it is about 1 percent, a reflection of the generally high income level of the population.

The school itself is a one-story building, quite small, fairly new, and beautifully situated in the midst of open fields, trees, and green hills. It is considered typical of the 120 schools in the county, many of which serve school populations of under a hundred children. An "infants and junior school," Bayford has an enrollment of seventy-six children between the ages of five and eleven in three classes, taught by three teachers and two assistants. The classrooms open off a large central room which is the school gym. It is in this room that lunch is served every day at noon to seventy-two of the seventy-six children in the school. Bayford, like every other school in the county, has its own kitchen. Here, it is next to the gym but separated from it by a counter on which the food is placed by the cook and her assistants. The meal is served from the counter to the children's tables by two "dinner ladies," women who live nearby, have children who attend neighboring schools, and work part-time for two hours each day, receiving a free meal.

At 11:45 each school day, the dinner ladies arrive, go over to one end of the gym where ten small tables and about eighty child-sized chairs are stacked, and proceed to distribute the tables around the room, eight chairs around each table. Then they set the tables: dinner plate, knife, fork, and spoon. No glasses are provided; water is not served at mealtimes so that the children will not fill up on it. Even the milk provided for the younger children is not served with meals. No napkins are provided; they are too expensive.

Earlier in the day, at 9:30, the school meals organizer–head cook and her two assistants, all of whom are local working-class wives and mothers, had begun preparation of the noon meal—a lamb casserole with carrots, peas, and potatoes, and lemon cake and custard for dessert.

They work quickly and efficiently in a kitchen the size of a large family's, with two ovens, six burners, and a small refrigerator barely adequate for keeping what is needed for the day's meal. Although menus are planned one week ahead and food is ordered weekly, it is delivered every day and no fresh food is kept overnight; leftovers are never served and food is not reheated. Stress is on cleanliness and nutrition more than aesthetics and taste; however, the resulting meal was both attractive and tasty and the clean plates of most of the children attested to their approval.

Promptly at noon, seventy-four shiny-faced and lively youngsters, somewhat curious about the stranger in their midst, trooped into the gym, stood quietly for a moment while grace was said, and then rushed to their respective tables. Although no formal places are assigned, the teacher supervising the dining room each day does try to ensure some mix of boys and girls at each table as well as a mix of younger and older children. Depending on whether or not a teacher or assistant teacher is present, seven or eight children are seated around each of the small, low tables. Although their presence is no longer required at mealtimes, the teaching staff all voluntarily accept dining-room supervision duty once a week, and two or three of them are usually present at mealtimes, eating informally with the children.

Seventy-two of the seventy-four children eating that day received the school meal. The other two brought sandwiches from home, in one case because the child is allergic to milk and milk products and the mother was worried about the child's diet, even though the school makes provision for special dietary needs. Children who bring lunch from home are permitted to sit at a table and eat with the others. Most parents pay for meals by check, on a weekly, monthly, or term basis; thus it is impossible to distinguish who pays and who does not, and both teachers and administrators work to keep it that way.

The meal begins when the dinner ladies carry platters or casseroles of food to each table, placing them in front of the child serving, usually one of the nine-to-eleven-year-old boys. The meal is served "family style," with the children passing their plates to the server at the head of the table. Each child has at least one turn at being server during the course of the term, but the older ones fill the role more often. Each child must take at least a little of everything offered, but the younger children usually request small portions and the older ones often ask for seconds. The self-assured competence and dexterity of a ten-year-old boy acting as the "father" at our table was most impressive. Yet equally delightful was the sight of a five year old, given the occasional honor of serving at his table, slowly and carefully spooning out portions as he served the older children and the teacher, proudly announcing "I didn't spill," while simultaneously reminding an eleven-year-old, "Don't forget. You must taste!" The sense of achievement the younger ones have after serving the group is enormous; one six-year-old boy proudly announced that visitors should have been present the day before when he had been server.

There is no choice of menu at this small school; however, children with special dietary needs (allergies, diabetes, obesity, religious scruples, or advance notice of particular dislikes) can be served something different. In general, the weekly menus are designed to respond to the children's current preferences; a new food that has been introduced is repeated or dropped from the menu according to the response. No bread is served at mealtimes, to avoid the children's filling up on starch instead of the more nutritious part of the meal. The emphasis is on protein content—"at least two meat meals per week" (beef or lamb), one fish, one poultry, one egg and cheese. Fresh vegetables and fruit are included regularly; puddings or custard are provided daily to ensure that the children have milk.

Even the smallest children feed themselves. Most eat with knives and forks, albeit slowly, with an occasional spilling on overalls; a few use spoons. When they first start school in the fall, many of the five year olds do have difficulty in using a knife and fork. Most try to emulate the older children around them and within a few weeks they manage quite well. But some continue to use spoons for a good part of the first year. No criticism is made of this either by teachers or by the other children. When we visited, two of the children were feeding themselves with spoons. At one other table a six year old was helping a "five" with his spoon. At another table an eleven-year-old girl was reminded by her little neighbor that she had promised to help her use a knife and fork; and help her she did, with great patience and tenderness, to be rewarded with an enormous smile as the little one demonstrated her newly learned skill.

At the beginning of the meal, one boy came to the teacher and said he had "a stomach ache." He was sent to another room to rest. When he reappeared a few minutes later to say he thought he might like to eat something, but wanted to eat in "the other room," no problem arose. He took his food from one table and carried it into the other room, ate it, and later rejoined the children, apparently having resolved his problem. Another little boy ate by himself in a corner of the room. He said that he "prefers eating alone," and the teacher said he'd been doing this since he had entered school that year and that when he was "ready" he would join the others. Again, no negative comments or criticism were made. Each child is assumed to be an individual and as long as his behavior does not disrupt the group he may follow his own pattern. The children who brought their own sandwiches ate at a table with others; again they evinced no discomfort and were obviously at ease with their friends, although eating differently.

The children giggled and chatted with one another, yet ate quickly, and by 12:30 all except one were finished. They stood up, said "thank you" to the "head," and rapidly scattered to get coats and go and play outside for the remaining hour of their lunch period. One youngster remained behind, her lunch still only half-eaten. It was explained that she is a "very slow eater," and she is permitted to finish at her own pace, without holding up the others, but again without any criticism.

Parents are free to visit the school at mealtimes whenever they wish, but this rarely occurs. There are occasional complaints from parents who say their children are vague about what they eat other than "meat and potatoes." Parents may phone and obtain specific information, but menus are not publicized in advance. We were interested to note that two days a week the same meal is also provided for nine elderly people living in nearby villages, as part of the local meals-on-wheels program. The current plan is eventually to provide meals five times a week for all the elderly living alone in the community.

School Meals in Two Large Urban Schools

Manchester, the fifth largest city in England, is an industrial city located in northern England, about 184 miles from London and two-and-one-half hours by train. It has a population of 616,520, including a diversity of ethnic and racial strains, a large group of poor, and many recently arrived immigrants.

We visited two schools in this city, the first an infants and junior school like the one mentioned earlier. Its current enrollment is just under four hundred children, divided into two sections: 180 infants aged five to seven and 215 juniors aged seven to eleven. Close to 70 percent of the children take school lunch and almost half of these are free. The school is brand new, opened within the past year, with classrooms all on one floor. It is located in what was described as "the largest slum clearance area in Europe," extending from the center of the city almost to its very edge. In an area in which buildings have been torn down and many new ones built, during the course of the past five years families have been dislocated, some have moved, and the turnover in children and variation in enrollment have been substantial, ranging from over five hundred in one year to less than three hundred in another, and four hundred in 1973. The surrounding community suffers from the usual indicia of poverty areas: high crime rates, filth, vandalism. In contrast to Bayford, this school has a very heterogeneous population, obviously much poorer; the children looked neither as clean nor as well cared for. Included among the students were a large number of Indian and Pakistani children, several blacks, and several others from a wide range of racial and ethnic backgrounds.

The current head of the school had been head of an older school in this community for twelve years. Although he liked some of the conveniences of the new building, he regretted the disappearance of a "separate dining room." A room used for only one hour a day, five times a week, is too expensive to be included in current school building plans, and most schools today use what are termed "dual-purpose facilities" for serving lunch. Assembly rooms, gyms, classrooms, corridors are all used to serve meals. Removing children from the room they are meeting or playing in, preparing the room for meals, cleaning up afterwards, all result in a certain amount of confusion and disorganization, especially in a large school with such a heterogeneous population.

Meals are provided in two sittings: the five to sevens eat from 11:45 to 12:15; then the tables are cleared, cleaned off, reset, for the seven to elevens, who eat between 12:30 and 1:00. Service here is family style also, with eight children at each table, served by the two children sitting at the head and to the right of the head. Meal supervision is rotated among the teachers, and again most teachers eat at least a few times a week with the children.

Because of the way this school was designed, with each classroom opening onto the outside as well as onto a wide central corridor which runs in a sort of zigzag fashion through the school building, children eat in five different areas, none of which is located next to the kitchen. The food is trundled to each area on "hot trolleys," like large rolling carts, by one of the dinner ladies, who then serves each table directly, placing the food in front of the server, who apportions it for each child.

All the children had the same meal, a beef casserole, with very small pieces of meat and vegetables, geared to the eating skills of the youngest children. Once again there was no choice: steak pie, potatoes, cabbage, and rice pudding. Observing 180 five to seven year olds serving each other—discussing how large or small the portions should be and who liked or did not like the dish, who was entitled to something "special"—

provided a remarkable illustration of independence, self-discipline, the social and technical skills involved in group eating, and patience and sensitivity in helping each other. Occasionally, one of the smallest, while eating with a spoon, would try out his skills with knife and fork. Sometimes, when frustrated, he would return to his spoon; at other times, dogged use of knife and fork continued. Some food ended up on faces, clothes, or tables, but the children's pleasure and pride in achievement were quite obvious.

In this school, a substantial percentage of the children received free meals. Although every effort is made to maintain anonymity, many of the young children are quite open about receiving free meals and no stigma seemed to be attached to it by either teachers or peers. When meal tickets are purchased each week, several children shout their "free" status that week. Children may declare their status on a short-term (one or two weeks) or longer basis. Sometimes, parents who are supposed to be paying for meals find themselves in financial straits and do not pay for several weeks or even months. Usually, the local education authority will work this out with parents, often "forgiving" such lapses where there is reasonable explanation.

Another school we visited in Manchester is a secondary "comprehensive" school opened in 1967. Here an equally heterogeneous group of about two thousand children, ranging in age from eleven to eighteen, are enrolled. Meals are provided in three different areas: one is for the eleven year olds, who are just making the transition from primary to secondary schools and for whom this large school represents a somewhat overwhelming new environment; the second, the main eating area, is a dining room in which nine hundred students eat in two shifts; the third is a special setting for the oldest, sixth-form "seniors," aged sixteen to eighteen. This last group eats in a separate facility that includes a lounge, record players, and television and offers certain privileges. Talking, dancing, playing records and guitars, long-haired and wearing casual clothes, they looked like an American teenage group. Their meals are self-service, although a thirty-cent meal is available, as well as a wide variety of other items. The canteen is subsidized and, of course, nonprofit, so prices are low. There is some concern that students should have an adequately nutritious meal; however, it is thought to be more important that they take their meals on the school premises. Occasionally, some school athletes who are concerned about getting an adequate and substantial meal at low cost may eat with the younger students in the regular school cafeteria.

In the rest of the school, eleven hundred students, over 60 percent of the total number enrolled, eat the school meal. In general, take-up of school meals tends to be lower for secondary-school students than for primary. About one-half of the students receive free meals. As mentioned earlier, the eleven year olds eat separately, in what is otherwise used as an assembly hall. At noontime, they all troop into the hall, rush toward a storeroom, and carry out and set up tables and chairs; then they set the tables themselves. All this is done quickly, efficiently, and relatively quietly. Here, too, tables are set for eight and service is family style, from the nearby kitchen, which also serves the main dining room.

Nine hundred students, divided into two sittings, eat in the school dining room in which tables are permanently set up. There is a long counter dividing the kitchen and the dining room; food is placed on the counter by the assistant cooks and then one person from each table, the main server for the day, picks up the food and brings it to his or her table. Although the students are not formally assigned to tables, there is a tendency for the same pattern of tables to be repeated, although positions at each table change daily. Again, the service is "family style," but three people serve: the person at the head of the table portions out the main dish, the one to his right serves the potatoes, and the one to the left other vegetables. Serving rotates on a clockwise basis, and each day the students move around the table so that the server changes from day to day. There is a choice of two dishes for each course. However, students must decide immediately what and how much they want; once the portions are served (and they can be of any size), the platters and serving dishes are returned to the counter. Seconds are not available, although variations in the size of portions are quite acceptable. "Chips" (french fried potatoes) are a favorite, as they are here; platters of these always return to the kitchen empty.

Eating at a table of fifth-form, fifteen-to-sixteen-year-old students was perhaps only a little more restrained than eating as a guest with a similar group in the United States. Both the girls and the boys had long hair and wore casual clothes, although one boy, obviously dressed for a visiting guest, wore jacket and tie. Their future plans ranged from becoming an architect or a teacher to entering the Royal Air Force or "just don't know." All had been eating school meals since they first entered school and said they would not have it otherwise since they like eating with friends. Half said this was in fact their main meal; they had a light supper or "tea" in the evening. Several others said that the family would have a large evening meal because there were younger children in the family who were not yet in school. Two boys said they were hungry again at night and needed and wanted two large meals.

The day's choice of main course was liver or pizza. Like American teenagers, all took pizza, followed by salad, french fries, carrots, and apple cake. In about fifteen minutes they all wolfed down a substantial meal.

Inevitably, the room was crowded and the din from 450 twelve to sixteen year olds all talking at once was overwhelming. Yet here, too, several teachers ate with the students. Although the visitor had been prepared for problems in this large group of teenagers, there was no rowdyism. There may have been constraint because guests were present, but they all seemed relaxed and in normal high spirits.

The kitchen staff consists of the young attractive woman who is the school meals organizer and head cook and her four assistants. The kitchen itself is large, with multiple cooking units and a large walk-in refrigerator. Again, there is no freezer, because food is prepared daily and no leftovers are kept, and no dishwasher, because it does not save staff and "it doesn't get dishes clean enough" (they are hand washed and submerged in boiling water to be sterilized). The kitchen was spotless even though eleven hundred meals had been prepared and served in ninety minutes.

Menus are prepared one month ahead (four school weeks) and great effort is made to please the children. Here, as in all other school kitchens, the woman in charge explained that "eating must be fun"— that it was as important that children enjoy what they ate and that the entire eating experience be pleasurable as that they had nutritious food. One assistant cook said she had been reassured about the meals her children had in school since she began working there. Another said that knowing her children had a good midday meal relieved her of the burden of cooking at night. Two others, as well as several at other schools, stressed the advantage of their work schedules, since the job enabled them to be home in the afternoon when their children came home from school (their working day is 9:00 to 3:00) and on all school holidays.

The London Scene

The inner London schools present a sharp contrast to schools visited elsewhere in England. A high percentage of the students are poor and an equally high percentage are nonwhite. In one such school, a major problem faced by the teachers is that of immigrant children who literally arrive in England on a Friday and show up in school on Monday. Bewildered when confronted in the school dining room by strange foods and, often, a strange language, the little ones react either by withdrawal or with disruptive, attention-seeking behavior which cannot easily be coped with in a half-hour, especially if the child is to eat as well. One teacher complained, "What can and should be a valuable learning and socializing experience, especially for the more deprived West Indian children, becomes a force-feeding marathon instead."

In another London school, the very youngest children, who attend only one half-day, are encouraged to go home at noon for their meals. Even when they start attending school on a full-time basis, their mothers are requested to feed them at home for the first few weeks until they acclimate to the school situation. This is not always possible because many, if not most, of the mothers work to supplement family income. Either they are not home at midday or, if they are, they know that the children can be fed better and more economically at school.

Secondary schools in London face still further problems: the large number of outside alternatives to eating at school, and the strong objections of the organized teachers' groups to adding the sometimes onerous burden of dining-room supervision to their already difficult tasks. Teenagers generally want and have more independence than younger children, and object to the constraints and limitations of the traditional school meal. Faced with sharply decreased numbers of students requesting the meal and complaints from the surrounding community about teenagers' rowdy behavior during the noon hour—buying food from street vendors, throwing remains around the sidewalk, shouting and running around—several schools decided to experiment with different types of meals to attract the students back to school. One such experiment is the "cash cafeteria" at Lavender Hill, an all-girls school in which 70 percent of the student body is nonwhite and over 60 percent of the students are entitled to a free meal. Each day the student can choose to have the regular school meal, the menu of which is posted on a board at the entrance to the dining room (which doubles as the school assembly hall). If it does not tempt her, she can join the cafeteria line. Most girls opt for the latter. Since everyone pays for lunch with thirty-cent vouchers, a girl entitled to a free meal uses her voucher to purchase food worth that amount while others may decide to eat more or make a more expensive choice, and then pay extra. During the ten or fifteen minutes it took more than a dozen girls to go through the cafeteria line and select food, the cash register rang only once. A few girls did say that the regular school meal increases in popularity toward the end of the week when pocket money is running low. Since the cash cafeteria had been initiated a year before, the number of girls taking school meals had more than doubled and, as an added benefit, the afternoon truancy rate had declined substantially.

One concern in instituting this new form of meal service is that, by permitting the students to eat what they wish, control over the nutritional content of the meal is eliminated. However, the girls seem to choose a reasonably well-balanced plate from the hot foods (hamburgers, hot dogs, meat pies), salads, cold meats, and delicious pastries and desserts. Several of the girls on the cafeteria line and at the tables spoke in favor of the cafeteria. Those few who were eating the traditional meal said their mothers preferred it, considering it more nutritious, but their mothers did not know which parts of the meal the girls either left on their plates or refused at the serving counter. The staff said that there is far less wastage when the students are free to choose. At present, 80 percent of the school meals served in London are cafeteria style, and only 20 percent are family service. This is in sharp contrast to schools visited in other parts of England.

Finally, the problem of inadequate dining-room supervision is a major concern in the London schools. Three years before our visit, the teachers scored a tactical success by having eliminated from their contract the right of the head, or school principal, to order them to take dining-room supervision duty. Since by law the headmaster of the school is responsible for school meals, often the only way he can obtain teacher participation is by personal pressure and influence. In some cases, the headmaster has to assume the supervision himself. For a variety of reasons—the schools are larger, the student body more heterogeneous, the teachers more organized, the turnover rate higher, and therefore the likelihood of a personal relationship with the head less—the London schools seem to have a much greater problem than schools elsewhere in England. The middle-aged, untrained women and elderly men now employed in supervisory duties are often overwhelmed by the behavior of hundreds of teenagers. London schools now run the grave risk of getting out of hand because staff is unable to control the children during the lunch hour, creating problems for teachers of afternoon classes. The frustrations of having to deal with the results of high spirits and lack of discipline at mealtime have caused some teachers to involve themselves in school lunch supervision again, but such participation is still minimal. Local government officials as well as some teachers hope that there may be some renegotiation of this issue of teacher supervision of the dining room, in return for teachers' receiving extra pay. Unfortunately, there is still no plan for this.

A government report on school meals has recently been completed, although it has not yet been made available to the public. The report includes recommendations regarding the content of the meals; improvement of the service and style of preparation; and the provision of additional non-midday meals (breakfasts, teas, snacks) for students attending extended sessions or beginning very early in the day. The thorny issue of dining-room supervision apparently has been avoided in that report and will continue to present a problem. Nevertheless, the school meals program is still defined by provider and recipients as an important component of Britain's educational system, and concern for its improvement and expansion continues.

School Lunch in the United States: The Reluctant Lunch Wagon

If we have portrayed school lunches in England with admiration and affection, it is not because we think there is nothing comparable in the United States.[1] We are sure we could find more than a few schools in the United States as impressive as the best in Britain. Furthermore, the British themselves are quite conscious of inadequacies in their program and are quick to point out such things as the invidiousness of stigma and the difficulty in completely eradicating it even though the authorities strive assiduously to avoid or at least minimize it; the horrendous effects of the current inflation and the consequent pressure on costs and prices of the school lunch; and the need for more rigorous enforcement of rules and regulations regarding nutritional content and standards, in the face of inadequate numbers of staff assigned to monitoring and regulatory duties.

A far sharper contrast might have been made if we had selected for description and comparison the Swedish school lunch program. Under its universal, totally free program, Sweden provides lunches at school for *all* children, at *no* cost to any. Menus appear in the daily press. The fact is, however, that although the British program is far from perfect, it provides a context in which we can analyze our own program and a modest standard against which to assess it.

The school lunch program in the United States has changed sub-

1. A good current source on school lunch in the United States is the *CNI Weekly Report*, published by the Community Nutrition Institute, 1910 Kay Street NW, Washington, D.C. 20006.

stantially within the last few years under congressional prodding with respect to the extent of federal financial support, federal policies regarding eligibility for free or reduced-price lunches, and the rate at which poor children participate in the program. When we first began looking at different types of European programs that help families, the disparity between the United States and the United Kingdom was enormous. The federal government subsidy was half of what it was in Britain (and of what it currently is in the United States). Eligibility was much more restrictive and coverage for poor children was far less extensive here than in the United Kingdom. Yet in spite of the recent changes in federal policies and the expansion of federal support, certain disparities still exist between the two countries. Certain issues are still unresolved in the United States; others have emerged more clearly.

During 1973–74, about fifty-one million children between the ages of five and eighteen were enrolled in school and about twenty-two million, or 43 percent, were served lunch in school. This figure represents a decline, both in absolute numbers as well as proportionately, over the last few years. We spend more than the British per-school meal ($.75); moreover, prices are disproportionately higher ($.46). On an overall basis, the payments cover about 37 percent of the cost of the program; about 23 percent comes from state and local governments, and 40 percent from the federal government.

Federal government guidelines permit children of families with incomes below 125 percent of the poverty income guidelines to obtain free lunch. Most schools, however, stick rather rigidly to the poverty income as the upper eligibility level. Census bureau estimates indicate that more than seven million children live in families with incomes below poverty level, while over ten million children qualify for the program under current maximum eligibility levels. Furthermore, eligibility for reduced-price lunches has been extended to children of families with incomes below 175 percent of the poverty guidelines. Yet only about 5 percent of this latter group is now receiving reduced-price school lunches. Here is the major take-up gap.

In all, seventeen million children—or more than one-third of the total number attending school—are eligible for free or reduced-price lunches, but less than half of those eligible are now taking advantage of this benefit and eating a school lunch. A major question for the United States is, why is participation in this program so low?

First, not all schools provide a "school lunch." Unlike Britain, where all schools are required by law to provide school meals, participation in the U.S. School Lunch Program depends on the initiative and decision of the individual school. Of the approximately 100,000 schools in the United States, at least 18,000 still do not participate. In some small schools, providing meals is too costly. In others, school boards refuse to participate because they believe that children should go home for lunch, even though the home may be empty and the mother at work. Some school administrators reject participation because they object to the bureaucratic confusion and complexity surrounding the program: the inadequacy, undependability, and insecurity of funding; the enormous numbers of papers required. Other schools do not participate because they have no food-service facilities; located in poverty areas, they have no money to purchase equipment, and the federal government provides only limited assistance. De facto discrimination against the poor is the result, since many of those most in need are thus excluded from any possibility of receiving lunch at school.

Second, not all children who are potentially eligible actually can or do avail themselves of this benefit. Eight million of those served in 1973–74 were poor children, receiving a free lunch; about 200,000 more received a reduced-price lunch. However, at least two million more equally poor children and over six million more eligible "near poor" and working-class children received no lunch at school. The reasons for this include differences in the maximum level for eligibility for the program, which may vary from community to community; whether or not a child attends a school that provides a school lunch; and the extent to which the stigma of receiving a free or reduced-price lunch may be so humiliating that the child would rather go hungry.

Critics allege that instead of publicizing the program, requiring school participation or at least encouraging it, and stimulating "take-up" by individual children, the primary concerns of the Department of Agriculture (USDA), the agency administering the program, would appear to be monitoring closely the number of children receiving free or reduced-price meals; avoiding what the USDA terms "fiscal abuse," that is, meticulously screening out those children who are ineligible, whose families' income is more than $4,510 for a family of four; and providing an outlet for federal surplus foods obtained through price supports in aid of farmers. In this context, the noted nutritionist Dr. Jean Mayer, speaking at a hearing of the Select Committee on Nutrition and Human Needs of the U.S. Senate (October 14, 1971), said that "as long as the School Lunch Program has as an avowed aim the accommodation of agricultural surpluses, we shall continue to have a poor program." Yet, at present, acute shortages of certain basic commodities have led the heads of several schools to comment that the children will soon be eating a lot of peanut butter sandwiches.

A further alleged indication of the weakness of the USDA's support of the program is the fact that its Food and Nutrition Service is unable to field a staff technically competent to assist states and school districts to increase the number of schools with programs or to operate and manage the overall program as a nutritional delivery mechanism. Technical assistance is limited for the most part to food matters dealing with menu design and content and cautionary materials on food handling and sanitation. The School Lunch Program has not yet given serious attention to the problem of nutrition education, even at a time when the inadequacies in the diets and eating habits of children and adults are receiving increasing study. Finally, no effort is made by the USDA to explore the reasons why children who are eligible for the program and are attending schools that do have a school lunch program do not participate. One recent survey of eligible students listed among their reasons: administrative errors rejecting their eligibility status; bureaucratic indifference; inadequacies in the program itself. No attempt has been made to explore these problems for more precise detail, to eliminate them, or even to institutionalize such monitoring and evaluation of the program by the department administering it.

In the United States today, the School Lunch Program is defined as a social service for poor children. A higher percentage of those eating school lunch in the United States, in contrast to Britain, are poor. However, one quarter of those identified as poor and 95 percent of those eligible for reduced-price lunches do not receive them; and most of those taking school meals are clearly from average, middle-class families. Of the total school population, including the millions of low- and middle-income pupils, the overall proportion of children taking lunch in Britain is more than 75 percent higher than in the United States. And neither the USDA nor most of the low-participation schools have made any large-scale efforts to publicize the program or explain the impact of changes in the law so as to make the program more widely available and more readily accessible to children.

Although the school is one of the two primary environments in which a child develops, providing lunch is not defined here as part of the overall educational program as it is in Britain. That is so in spite of the fact that many educators and other professionals emphasize school lunch as aiding in the socialization and training of young children and facilitating informal relationships and interactions between teachers and students and among students of different ages.

Everyone agrees that a good and nutritious meal is essential for the development of a healthy child, and one idea behind the program is that the meal should provide one-third of a child's daily nutritional needs. Furthermore, growing awareness of poor eating and food-buying habits —exacerbated by rising costs of food—has led to increased recognition of the importance of nutrition education. Yet, the School Lunch Program is not defined as a health service.

Finally, although women are working in increasing numbers, and households at all income strata are often empty during the middle of the day, some people still persist in the obsolete and unrealistic belief that all children are or should be eating lunch at home.

In the last few years a growing number of professionals, lay people, and organizations have recommended that the federal government establish a universal free school lunch program for all children, and that, until such a program can be implemented, priority should be given to the poor and near-poor children. Yet, in 1972, the USDA prohibited the state of West Virginia from conducting the most progressive school lunch program in the country, whereby any child under the eligibility standard received a free lunch and *all* other children regardless of their financial situations received a reduced-price meal. The idea of universalism is also rejected by some people who are truly concerned about poor children and who worry that the cost of a universal school lunch program would deflect needed resources from other types of provision for poor children. Recently, several communities refused participation in the school lunch program out of fear that it would increase the movement of "poor people" into their communities. Others not only remained out of the program but suspended children who brought their own lunches to school.

The U.S. School Lunch Program has expanded over the past five years. However, between present realities and a program of daily nutrition and group socialization for all American schoolchildren there are the following: confused, inconsistent, and occasionally conflicting policies regarding eligibility, provision, and function; continued existence of stigma, even at the level of school authorities, related to receiving a free meal; limited recognition of a sharply growing trend among mothers of school-aged children to work during the day, thus necessitating provision of lunch at school for the child; failure to incorporate a continuous monitoring and evaluation of the program, especially with regard to the generally low level of take-up and the known problems in the program; inadequate efforts at publicizing availability of the program and ensuring access to it; and, finally, inadequate stress on the comprehensive nutritional focus of the program, and failure to recognize the essential importance of providing good nutrition *and* nutrition education for children. Surely these matters require debate, resolution—and action.

4

Housing for the Young and Single

in France and Denmark

IN the last several years a new group, the "young singles," has emerged in the United States and has received increasing attention. Los Angeles, long given up to youth culture and a magnet for the "young and attractive," was the first city to demonstrate the appeal of apartment complexes designed for the young and unattached. Other cities followed soon after, constructing multiple-housing units, boasting a wide range of social facilities such as swimming pools and tennis courts, limited to "singles" only. "Bachelor Party" tours, cruises, and special resort weekends are advertised to meet the needs of the young (and sometimes not so young) who live alone and are searching for companionship. Resorts have been designed specifically for singles, and recently several country clubs have been established for similar purposes. The newspapers are full of advertisements for residential complexes, social clubs, dances, vacation resorts, and so forth—all designed to attract this group.

Although it began as an urban phenomenon, the burgeoning growth of such developments has now taken place in a variety of suburban communities. Unquestionably, private enterprise has identified a potential pot of gold in these young middle- and upper-class consumers, who are now living on their own in increasing numbers, getting married later, and earning higher salaries. Even this brief description of the kinds of facilities and services now available shows that in the United States the market has already responded to the more affluent sector of this group, but exploration leads rapidly to the conclusion that there are no parallel developments for lower- and working-class youths.

But how large a group really falls into the category of young people living on their own, and whom are we really talking about? Census figures indicate that in 1972 there were 42.4 million youths aged fourteen to twenty-four, representing 20.3 percent of the population, a 56 percent increase since 1960. Of these, 55 percent are in school and 42 percent are working. Interestingly enough, even among those attending school, 18 percent of college students aged twenty to twenty-one and 47 percent of those aged twenty-two to twenty-four live in their own households rather than in dormitories or with parents or relatives. Of course, most of those who are working live on their own.

The European situation with regard to the young and unattached differs from the American in two noteworthy ways. First, although the trend toward increased numbers in this group is similar to ours, the percentage who are single and living alone is smaller, at least in some countries. For example, France has a population of eight million youths between the ages of fifteen and twenty-four, seven million of whom are single. Of these, 4,000,000 are workers, 2,500,000 are students, and 350,000 are in military service, but only about 900,000 live alone. However, a recent government survey revealed that one-third of those still living with their parents would prefer to live on their own and would do so—if adequate and reasonable accommodations were available. Second, and of particular interest, is the fact that in several countries, perhaps because the demand is smaller, the private sector still has not responded to the needs of this group in any substantial fashion. Instead, it is the public sector and the national governments who have initiated a variety of programs addressing the needs of the young, single worker. Types of provision vary from country to country; some may be less relevant to American youth than others; and we have by no means managed in our survey to cover the whole range of provision. What follows is a brief description of two very different approaches to providing housing for young, single workers which indicate contrasting governmental efforts at meeting this newly defined social need of "ordinary" citizens.

Young Workers' Homes in France

Although there have been homes for young workers in France since the beginning of the twentieth century, current developments date from immediately after World War II. Before this, concern for young workers was the exclusive province of religious organizations, especially private Catholic philanthropy and, to a much smaller extent, Protestant groups. After the war, an accelerated exodus occurred from rural to urban areas in France, with millions of young people leaving their homes to find work in major urban and industrial centers. While the cities offer work to the young and unattached, a recent study of this population, made at the instigation of the government, indicates that adequate and reasonable housing facilities continue to be their most pressing need once jobs are obtained. Although only 20 percent of the young single workers live away from home, another 27 percent would live alone if satisfactory accommodations were available. When asked what kind of housing they want, they pick individual, single-bedroom units with cooking facilities, where they can entertain friends in their rooms and come and go as they please, at rents they can afford on the salaries they earn.

The solution for many is homes for young workers. With reasonably comfortable accommodations, less expensive than any comparable form of lodging, providing companionship and camaraderie, these homes provide a transition for the young who are moving from family living to total independence.

According to the Ministry of Public Health, the responsible governmental authority, a young workers' home is defined as "a nonprofit organization, the purpose of which is to assure young, single workers between the ages of fourteen and twenty-five, lodging and food, cultural activities, and a socioeducational experience." A recent census indicates that as of 1973 there were 613 young workers' homes in all of France: 233 for males; 286 for females; and 94 that are "mixed" or coed. They total 55,300 beds: 5,800 in Paris, 9,000 in the environs of Paris, and 40,500 in the provinces.

The homes accept as residents apprentices and industrial and white-collar workers, regardless of income, as long as they can pay the monthly rental, which is generally about $110 per month for room and two meals a day (and $80 monthly for studio accommodations and no meals). In addition, a maximum of 20 percent of the residents may be students at technical and vocational schools. For the most part, however, students are not encouraged to use these homes because their different values and the fact that they are not earning their own living often lead to conflict with the young workers. Furthermore, many of the students have alternative residences—university-related housing—even though many object to these accommodations just as our own college students do.

Young foreign workers are also accepted in these homes, but on a limited basis. Rarely will any home accept more than a maximum of 20 percent of foreign residents; again, the tensions that arise between young Frenchmen and a larger foreign group tend to create problems. However, with the inevitable increase in the number of young workers from member EEC countries, the French government recognizes that more accommodations will be needed. Present facilities, inadequate even for the existing French demand, cannot begin to meet these needs.

Finally, a limited number of young people on probation, who are referred by the court or by a social agency, and some physically handicapped youngsters are also accepted.

In principle, the homes are designed for young people between the ages of fifteen and twenty-five. In fact, each home decides itself what age range to concentrate on. Thus, some are primarily for those aged sixteen to twenty-one, others for those aged eighteen to twenty-five, and some few accept residents up to the age of thirty, although by law the limit is twenty-five. Most homes strive to maintain at least one-fourth of their residents in the under-twenty-one age category, since this group is defined as most in need of such facilities.

Homes are established under both public and voluntary auspices: municipalities, construction industries, chambers of commerce, the quasi-public agency that distributes family allowances, or charitable organizations. Thirty percent of the homes belong to religious congregations but are open to all youths regardless of religious convictions. All auspices are nonprofit, except where a business organization is involved in initiating the development of a home only for its own workers.

Although, in theory, a careful study is made of the need for a home before it is built, such studies tend to be casual. On occasion, the result may be a home built in a community with inadequate employment opportunities, or in an area with limited access to public transportation. All surveys of occupancy rates of young workers' homes demonstrate that homes situated in areas of full employment, with ready physical access to work, are fully occupied and usually have waiting lists. Others may be half empty.

In order to obtain financial assistance for construction from the government, the home must adhere to certain regulations as specified by law: (1) Homes for young workers must have a maximum capacity of 150 beds. If most of their tenants are over eighteen, then they may be comprised of two units of 150 beds. (2) If the homes are to be lived in by youth of both sexes, the residents must be accommodated in separate parts of the lodging, with access by separate stairs. (3) The measurements of the rooms must have minimum and maximum footage as follows: a room for one person must have a minimum of 12 square yards and a maximum of 14; one for two persons must have a minimum of 16 square yards and a maximum of 20; and a room for three persons must have a minimum of 21 square yards and a maximum of 25. (4) Each room must have a bed, a toilet with sanitary facilities and running water, and a wardrobe that has space equal to 2 square feet. (5) Each floor of rooms must have showers, at least one for every ten residents, and one group of toilets for ten residents maximum. And (6) the precise regulations must take into account the following collective facilities: a kitchen and a restaurant, a group meeting room, a leisure room and a cafeteria, a reception and a waiting room, and an administrative room and general service room.

Financial assistance itself may be in the form of direct public subsidies or grants from one of several agencies, in an amount up to 15 percent of the construction costs, and/or subsidized interest payments on mortgages. At present, construction costs average about $5,000 "per bed."

The program represents the coordinated efforts of both public and voluntary organizations, with strong support in construction costs from the government or from the national office for family allowances. In addition, the government often subsidizes a portion of the salaries of the *animateur* or youth worker. Some homes receive a small amount of assistance from the municipality, a general advisory council, big business, or a similar source, but these are quite minimal and usually short term. Except for such occasional small grants, no subsidies are available to defray the expenses of maintaining the homes, expenses which have risen sharply in the last few years.

The home is administered by a paid director who is the operational head of the home; when the home has more than fifty residents, there is also an assistant director. This staff is responsible for all administrative and financial matters. Each home having at least one hundred residents will also have an *animateur* to act as "group leader." Directors and *animateurs* may be social workers, former teachers, or untrained people who have had experience in working with young people. They are given some brief, focused training for this work. Finally, there are technical and custodial staff.

Each residence has an unpaid voluntary board composed of lay and professional people, and sometimes also of residents, who make policy for the home (age range of residents, composition of residents, rules regarding social behavior). The National Union of Homes for Young Workers makes the broad policy decisions, but specific individual policies are left to the management and the board of each home. For each of the twenty-one regions of France, the homes elect one representative (either director or chairman of the board) and one alternate. Three additional representatives come from the Paris region and one more from Lyon. In all, this group of twenty-five plus delegates from the various federations (Catholic, Protestant, Communist, socialist, trade union, etc.) constitutes a national administrative council for the young workers' homes. This council elects a nine-member bureau or committee of directors who constitute the primary advisory council to the homes. Although its function is primarily that of providing information, identifying trends, doing research, developing cooperation, and influencing policy in the government, it also sets the rentals.

In effect the physical facility is subject to central government regulations. The committee of directors sets overall charges and general policy guidelines and constraints; the individual residence's policy board decides on the specific regulations for each home and oversees costs and general maintenance. Finally, within each home an in-house advisory council, composed of residents and staff, decides on house rules, the organization of leisure activities, and the financial aspects of these activities.

As of 1973, the average cost for accommodations and two meals per day was $110 per month. Almost all young workers pay their own expenses; however, since 1971 a small percentage of the cost has been defrayed by public assistance for very low-income youths without families, or whose families also have low incomes, and for youths entering a home before finding a job. (This latter is something like a short-term, three-month loan.)

To American eyes, the French young workers' homes look like a cross between college dormitories, YMCA's, and hotels for women. Yet there is enough range among these facilities to provide some interesting examples of how to house young people, even though some aspects of the French experience seem less relevant for us than others. The three young workers' homes described below illustrate the somewhat different approaches France takes to this special housing need.

L'Accueil is a modern, multistory building, completed in 1966 and located in a working-class suburb about a ten-minute train ride from Paris. It is unusual in that it includes housing for the aged as well as for young workers. In fact, it was originally developed, designed, and financed by the local municipality specifically for the aged. Only because sufficient space was available on the designated site was a decision made to include housing for young workers also. Because of this combined function, the municipality contributes some financial support to the young workers' home, contrary to the usual practice.

The building is divided into two wings, separated on the first floor by a core of communal living and eating facilities. One wing includes studio apartments (bedroom/living room, kitchenette, bath) for thirty-five elderly people aged seventy-eight and over. The other wing includes 130 single rooms without private baths (each floor contains twenty such rooms, six toilets, and six showers) for young women between the ages of sixteen and twenty-five. A separate building constructed in 1972 has 175 pensioners' flats (studio apartments for the elderly), accommodating a "younger" elderly population, those seventy to eighty, who also use the communal facilities of the main building.

Since the young workers' accommodations have no cooking facilities, breakfast and dinner are provided by the home. Although the pensioners' flats have such facilities, restaurant meals are available for those who do not wish to cook, and for their friends, relatives, and guests. There is one main kitchen serving both wings of the home. However, off the kitchen are two separate dining facilities: one a dining room where individual tables are set, a menu provided, and the meal served to the older residents; the other an informal cafeteria where the young residents serve themselves from a counter connected to the kitchen. About thirty of the elderly have either lunch or dinner in the restaurant, while approximately one hundred girls eat dinner only there. Both restaurants are open to the neighboring community, but the prices for meals are higher for nonresidents. In addition to the restaurant facilities, two communal living rooms are also located on the main floor. Some social interchange does occur here between the two groups of residents, but it is the young rather than the older people who are more likely to make the overtures. Besides these basic communal facilities, several others are located on each floor. Among these are a sewing room, an ironing room, a laundry with electric washing machines and dryers, a television room, a library, and a room with electric hair dryers. There is also a small "infirmary" for each wing, though these are rarely used. The director of the home, who administers both wings, said that since there is no resident doctor or nurse, any resident who is really ill is immediately sent to the nearby hospital.

Like all such homes situated in communities with close to full employment, where unskilled and semiskilled jobs are readily available, this home is fully occupied and there is a short waiting list. The monthly rate for a room, dinner, and breakfast (meals for twenty-five days per month, since most of the girls go away on weekends to visit either relatives or friends) is about $90; the average salary for these workers is about $250 monthly. No variations in rental are provided in relation to differences in wages, a great source of concern to the directors of many homes, since this rental, fixed by the overall organization of homes, effectively excludes the lowest wage earners. A charge of about 40 percent of average salary for rent and two meals a day is typical for most young workers' homes in France. Yet, even with what the French describe as relatively high prices for accommodations—prices which are somewhat exclusionary—and despite additional assistance provided by the municipality, L'Accueil, like many other homes, is running with a deficit. Part of the explanation apparently is that only a small percentage of construction costs may be provided by the government. While the government assists in obtaining construction loans and mortgages and subsidizes interest payments, all maintenance charges—taxes, utilities, general maintenance and administration—must be paid as if the home were a private facility.

The young women living at L'Accueil are mostly between the ages of sixteen and twenty-one, although about one-third are older. The home has stringent rules about not permitting male visitors above the first floor and requires that the girls always leave word if they are going away overnight or for the weekend. Several of the girls we interviewed objected to these rules and said that as soon as they could find other accommodations they would leave. The social constraints may be one reason why the residents in this home tend to be younger than in some of the less "traditional" homes we visited.

Yet the home is full; there is a waiting list for accommodations, and the residents seemed happy and relaxed. In general, the average stay at the home is about one year. After talking with several girls, we became convinced that the home served their needs, even if only on a brief and transitional basis. One tall, slender girl with carefully made-up large blue eyes, no lipstick, and straight blond hair hanging down to the middle of her back, looking very much like her American counterpart, explained that her parents lived far away in the provinces, where there were few jobs available, and so she had come to Paris to look for work —and perhaps "meet a young man." She had arrived in Paris a few months before and moved into a small, dark room in a decrepit building, in a "bad" neighborhood. Although she had found a job in an office fairly easily, she was increasingly depressed and lonely. A fellow worker mentioned the home to her; while she found it restrictive, it was clean, attractive, cheap, and provided congenial friends. But now, after six months in residence, she and two of her friends were waiting to move into one of the "less traditional" homes.

Like Jeanne, most of the young women we interviewed came from the outlying provinces. Similarly, most saw this residence as transitional, to be lived in briefly until they got married, could afford a room of their own in a "decent place," could find an apartment to share with friends, or could obtain a place in a "preferred" residence.

The Residence Aramis, located in a working-class neighborhood in the twentieth arrondissement of Paris, is identified by young women in many of the homes as just such a residence. Fully occupied since it opened, this residence has the longest waiting list of any visited, and several young women interviewed at other homes said they had been waiting eight months for accommodations here. Admission to the residence is almost exclusively by referral from an employer. Most of the young women have already lived at other residences in Paris or elsewhere in France and seek out this home because of its greater freedom.

A nine-story building, constructed in 1972, it is described by its director as a "nontraditional" residence. By this she means that although it is a home for women only, residents are free to have both male and female guests visit in their rooms, and each room has a convertible chair that opens up into a bed, for putting up overnight guests. Although a quarter of the residents are between the ages of twenty and twenty-one, and close to one-third are between twenty-four and twenty-five, the home is unique in that almost half are between twenty-five and thirty. The women living here are particularly enthusiastic about the facility. However, the average stay is relatively short, about three to six months; most leave to get married or move into their own apartments.

The home has accommodations for 110 residents in studio apartments—a small bedroom with a bed, convertible club chair, and desk, a kitchenette with a two-burner range and small refrigerator underneath, a shower, a bidet, and a closet. Each floor has thirteen such studios as well as three toilets and one bathtub. In contrast to L'Accueil, where the keys are kept at the central reception desk, this residence is run much more like a French apartment house. Each resident has her own key; the director (like a concierge in some ways) will accept messages, but she does not expect to be kept informed of anyone's comings and goings. Rentals are $75 monthly, without meals.

There is no common dining room in this facility and all meals are prepared by the young women in their own apartments. As a consequence, many said they missed the opportunity for meeting other residents that communal eating facilities provide. A communal kitchen and two small dining rooms are available for use when guests come and may be reserved in advance for this purpose. Other communal facilities include a television room, a couple of lounges, a laundry, and a sewing room. As at L'Accueil, most of the young women come from outside

Paris and see this residence as a means of transition to living on their own. Attractive, inexpensive, and with few constraints, it eases the adjustment from life in a small town to life in a large and complex city. Most of the young women have already lived on their own in similar residences, so the adjustment needed is of a special nature. Here the need is to learn how to handle complete freedom. Since this occasionally presents problems, a counsellor (*animateur*) is available to discuss personal problems.

In making their decision to move to this home, several of the young women were influenced by precisely this desire to achieve greater personal independence. Several had parents who lived in suburbs of Paris. One of these, Lucienne, explained that at twenty-two she resented the constraints of family life and the lack of privacy permitted her. She wanted to be "on her own." Her parents had objected initially but eventually agreed on condition that she would live in a "residence." Aramis was a mutually agreed upon compromise.

Like Aramis and L'Accueil, the men's residences in France may differ in living arrangements but tend to be impersonal in the attitudes expressed by management toward the residents. In contrast, one residence that is unusual for the concern and commitment the staff show for the youths is located in an industrial city about a hundred miles north of Paris. Again, it is a fairly recently constructed multistory building with single-room accommodations for 180 young men between the ages sixteen and twenty-five. About half are under twenty-one, a percentage that the director works hard to maintain since he feels that it is the younger boys who are most in need of protected living facilities. The monthly rate for a room and three meals per day is $120; with two meals (breakfast and dinner) the rate is $90. Since many of the residents work nearby, returning to the home for lunch is not unusual. The average salary for unskilled workers in this area is about $300 per month. In general, the average stay in the home is about one year. However, about 5 percent remain in the community even after they leave, and continue to remain involved with the home, its policies, and the new residents.

This building, too, is modern and has large communal facilities on the main floor, including a cafeteria. Breakfast is served here from 4:00 to 8:30 A.M. in order to take care of those residents who are working a wide range of shifts and schedules; lunch is served from 12:00 to 1:00 except for those who inform staff in advance that their work schedule permits a lunch break only between 2:00 and 3:00; dinner is served from 7:00 to 8:00 P.M., although again hot food is available until

10:30 for those who give prior notice. There are also several small lounges, television rooms, a "bar," a "discotheque" built by the residents themselves, and a large meeting room. All the facilities are heavily utilized.

Avoiding both the strict, protective formality of some residences and the impersonal hotel-like quality of others, this home is more like a college fraternity house. Although each residence has for its administrative core at least a director and an *animateur* (or group worker/community organizer), at no other did we find such active, involved, and committed leadership. In looks, dress, and behavior, it was hard to separate staff from residents; all were long-haired, wore blue jeans or corduroys and turtle-neck sweaters.

Intensely committed to the residents, the administrative personnel make a point of actively recruiting young people who they feel are particularly in need of semiprotected housing. Although they insist that it is essential that about half the residents be ordinary French working-class youth, so that the population of the home not be "tipped" in the direction of any particular group, they are equally insistent that residences such as these have a special obligation to accommodate the "hard to house"—foreign laborers, youths on probation, the physically handicapped. The composition of the residence thus reflects a deliberate effort on the part of the director to maintain a balance between "average young workers" and those with special needs, with limited inclusion of boys from "restricted categories." The residence therefore tends to include, in a total of 180, about thirty who are on probation, twenty "foreigners," and about five who are physically handicapped. The director was quite explicit about the function of such a residence: "It is to provide an environment in which boys can be socialized into acceptable adult roles, in which they can learn to be increasingly independent, learn how to take care of themselves, relate to the world of work, and obtain help and support from their peers and others, when they need it."

Each home must follow certain regulations set by the overall organization, but apart from rental charges, most of these relate to design and construction of the facility and to its maintenance. The homes have autonomy as to rules and regulations about the residents' composition and behavior.

Although in theory residents are included in making policy and house rules and regulations in all homes, this was the only one in which such participation seemed to be implemented substantially in fact as well as in theory. Since most turnover of residents occurs in the early fall of each year, elections for officers and members of the committee that administers the home are held then. An active group of current residents in addition to one or two former residents determines such policies as whether or not young women can visit the youths' rooms ("yes" for an hour or so, "no" for overnight visits); which newspapers the home should order ("yes" to left and right wing papers, "no" for an Arab language paper); when and with whom to hold dances; whether or not to invite the community at large to the home's monthly movies and, if nonresidents are invited, what to charge. In addition, the residents run their own "bar" and game rooms and set the prices; the proceeds go into a special fund used to purchase additional equipment (a television, a movie projector).

The residents are openly enthusiastic about the home, the staff, and each other. Great stress is placed on "mutual help" among residents and between staff and residents. A bulletin board is well located on the main wall of the central hall and up-to-date information is posted there about government benefits and services to which residents may be entitled. Staff are readily available to advise and counsel as needed. In addition, if it seems necessary, outside professional help may be made available.

One eighteen year old was referred to this residence by the court. He had killed his father while trying to protect his mother from repeated beatings. Working in close cooperation with court personnel, the staff have been involved in helping him learn to understand what happened and make an adjustment to normal life again. After two years at the home, he now has a job and is planning to leave the residence and return to his own home.

François, another eighteen year old, has been in residence for about one year. He left home when his parents separated and family conflict was so intense that he felt he could not live with either parent. He got a job in a nearby factory, but, as a minor, needed a semiprotected place to live. After a year, he is one of the leaders in the home, involved in several committees and all activities.

Jean, a long-haired, bearded, attractive but rather vulnerable-looking young man dressed in a blue checked shirt and grey flannel pants, has braces on both legs and cannot walk without crutches as a result of childhood polio. One year ago, when he was twenty-two, he and his parents discussed the importance of his learning how to live more independently, and perhaps obtaining some sort of training for work. There were no sheltered workshops near his home; however, his parents discovered there was one near this residence and so he applied for admission and was accepted. Because the wages paid him in the sheltered workshop are very low, he receives financial aid from the Assistance

Familiale (a French public assistance program). Interviewing Jean in his neatly kept room, a bright red and green plaid blanket thrown across his bed, pictures of his family and girl friend arranged on the shelf behind, we asked him about how he liked the home. With great enthusiasm he spoke of his friends—the *animateur* and certain other residents—and of his pleasure in living "on his own." With some sadness he expressed concern for his future. At twenty-five he must leave the residence. He did not look forward to returning to living with his family and hoped to find an alternative.

The three residences described above illustrate the fact that, unlike American singles housing, French homes are designed to meet a "need" rather than a "demand." Partly for this very reason, in recent years two aspects of the program have stimulated concern and debate in France. First, as the costs of maintaining these residences have increased, monthly rentals have also risen. This inflationary spiral has trapped the lowest-income workers. In effect, the program is increasingly "creamed" by the lower-middle-class worker. Although the individual directors are all concerned about this, none has been able to maneuver around the requirement for a minimum charge of about $110, depending on local variations in expenses. Most would like to implement a graded rental scale, but as long as the minimum is set by law to cover actual costs, the lowest-income workers, who may be the ones most in need, are automatically excluded from these facilities.

Second, a steadily growing number of the young are moving away from their homes and one-third of those between the ages of fifteen and twenty-four who are still living at home are believed ready to move out if accommodations were available. Although some homes are not full, for reasons mentioned earlier, space now available for young workers is nowhere near adequate to meet even present demand. Current plans project an additional 35,000 beds by 1980; but the French have begun to recognize that the approach now employed for housing young workers is only a first step in meeting this need.

For almost all homes, the turnover of residents is rapid and stays rarely exceed one year; often they are shorter. Although some get married and establish their own homes, and some young men leave to enter military service, most residents leave because they want and are ready for more independence. Unfortunately, their search for small apartments at low rentals continues to be frustrating and many settle for inadequate accommodations in dilapidated buildings or run-down neighborhoods, in order to avoid the institutional image and atmosphere of the young workers' homes. Inevitably, there are subsequent problems; and increasingly the French recognize this and accept responsibility for finding additional solutions. At present, there is growing pressure for the government to provide assistance—through construction or subsidized rentals—in obtaining small apartments in buildings serving families generally. In other words, the suggestion is that buildings containing apartments for ordinary families with children should also contain small units and some supplementary services for young people living alone or with one other person, where they can make the next transition to normal adult living in comfortable, clean quarters at rents they can afford.

Thus, after extensive experience with young workers' homes, the French now appear to be moving toward a two-tier approach to providing housing for youth: the first, semiprotected; the second, independent. Whether or not they will actually implement this approach, and when such provision will be made, remains to be seen.

Housing the Young in Denmark

The Danish experience in housing youth begins where the French leaves off: the Danes have initiated socially integrated housing for all ages, and one aspect of this is housing for single youths. Specifically, the government strongly encourages builders of new multiple-dwelling housing to provide a certain amount of space for youth between the ages of fifteen and twenty-four who are living on their own. If housing facilities are "approved," the government will partially subsidize interest payments on mortgages. Some portion of maintenance expenditures will be financed also, partly by the government and partly by local authorities.

Along with several other social developments, interest in and concern for unattached youths was stimulated by the experiences of World War II. A Youth Commission was appointed in 1945 which has influenced subsequent developments in this field. One of the commission's major concerns was identification of the special housing needs of single youths and the recommendation that some provision be made for meeting these needs within a normal residential environment.

This recommendation was first implemented in the early 1960s through the construction of a 1,000-unit public housing development containing individual bedrooms and communal living and eating facilities for fifty young people. A few years later, the second, nonprofit, multiple-housing complex was completed, containing 250 single rooms, called "dens," and several related communal facilities, specifically designed for unattached youths.

In this context, in order to stimulate similar initiatives in all new public housing and expand this type of provision generally, the National Society of Ungbo was founded in 1966. Composed of representatives of municipalities, the joint organization of Danish nonprofit building societies, trade unions, savings banks, and other concerned organizations as well as individuals, this society was established specifically to create housing for unattached children and youths—those with problems as well as average youths—regardless of socioeconomic background. A "congress" made up of two delegates from each affiliated organization as well as one delegate for each fifty "dens" elects a chairman and executive committee; these, in turn, appoint a director who becomes the person responsible for the daily operations of the society.

Ungbo implements its mission of promoting the welfare of young people by creating housing facilities which meet their special needs. It accomplishes this by encouraging the Danish building societies (most of which are nonprofit, are responsible for the initiation of most multiple-dwelling construction, and receive various forms of government subsidies) to include such facilities when constructing large-scale housing projects. Ungbo then rents this space from the building societies, assuring them of continuous financial responsibility, and rerents the apartments directly to young people who meet certain predefined criteria of need.

As of 1972, Ungbo had more than 2,500 "dens" in twenty-odd different housing developments, most built between 1966 and 1972 in the area surrounding Copenhagen. Rentals for these accommodations vary from $50 to $130 depending on size (with or without kitchenette or private bath) and number of meals provided (no meals or one, two, or three per day). Almost all residents pay their own way, although some assistance may be available for those with recognized financial need. Rooms are fully furnished, with bed, chairs, desk; but residents may bring their own furniture if they wish, or select other furniture. All accommodations have easy access to automatic laundry facilities, television rooms, and lounges, and often to cafeterias and kitchen facilities. Finally, all facilities are coeducational and men's and women's rooms are often adjacent. Residents over eighteen may have guests of either sex visit overnight; those under eighteen must have their parents' or guardians' permission to do this; for those seventeen and over, such permission is usually granted.

Each group of dens in a housing project is autonomous, to the extent that rentals are set by the individual "den division" to cover expenses (rentals of rooms and other communal facilities); and rules regarding residence composition (number of young men and women, ages of residents, number of "problem youths"), residents' activities, behavior, and so forth are set by the youths and staff of that facility. Social workers are assigned to these facilities to advise and counsel youths as necessary. Their salaries are paid by various public welfare agencies. Approximately one full-time social worker is assigned to every hundred youths. Most such counseling tends to be about budget management, employment, assisting residents who wish to move out of the "den," and general information, advice, and referral services.

The Danish approach to housing these young people seems particularly interesting to an American observer, and perhaps more relevant to our life style and experience than the French version. Responding to the growing number of young people living away from their families, the Danes aim at supporting this desire for independence in a context of a normal living environment. In fact, the primary objective is to provide living facilities for those older adolescents and youths wanting and needing some opportunity for greater privacy and independence in living, whose own families—usually working-class families—reside in the same large housing developments. Thus, in each new housing project containing accommodations for the young and single, priority is given to children of residents. Although this group may not be large initially, once accommodations are available and the residents become aware of this, the demand grows rapidly. In particular, for families with young children, demand grows with their children. For example, in one project completed in the late 1960s, initially only one or two rooms were occupied by such children. Four years later, in 1972, one-third of the rooms were occupied by children whose families lived in the housing complex; and the proportion continues to rise.

Typical of this group is nineteen-year-old Paul, the oldest of three children. His family has lived in a large suburban housing project just outside Copenhagen for the past four years. Since finishing high school, he has worked as an apprentice at a nearby factory. When he lived at home he would invite friends over to his home some evenings; but he shared a room with his two brothers and there were constant arguments over who could use the record player, how loud the music could become before his parents complained, and so forth. Often, in frustration, he went out in the evening looking for someplace to meet friends. His mother complained because he came home late, refused to say where he had been, and was generally uncommunicative.

For over a year tension mounted steadily between Paul and his parents—and between his mother and father regarding how to handle the conflict. One of Paul's friends, who was living in a den in the project, suggested that Paul send in an application to Ungbo. He did and was interviewed subsequently by the social worker and director of the den division in his project. Since Paul's problems were defined as "normal for adolescence" and his parents live in the housing complex, his need for a room was given priority. As soon as space was available, Paul was assigned a room. Although the accommodations are always full, turnover is fairly high; as in the French facilities, the average stay is about a year although it ranges from three months to three years.

Paul lives in a studio apartment (bedroom, bath, and kitchenette), one of several situated on the ground floor in one of the complex's eight buildings. He takes care of his own apartment, markets, and prepares most of his own meals, in addition to keeping up with work responsibilities. Occasionally, he takes dinner at a cafeteria serving the den residents in another building. He supports himself completely on the small salary he earns, even though initially he had some difficulty managing. One of the two social workers assigned to service these 250 dens helped him devise a monthly budget. At present, he is very enthusiastic about his living arrangements, as are his parents. He visits his family frequently, joining them for dinner once or twice a week. With his increased independence has come a concomitant assumption of domestic responsibilities. Since living on his own, he has recognized how much was done for him when he lived at home, and he acknowledges this freely. Conflict between him and his parents has decreased. When he does visit, he is far more communicative; his relationship with both his parents and his brothers has improved.

Another group of dens is located in a large 1,700-unit housing project ten minutes out of Copenhagen. This complex includes pensioners' flats (apartments for the elderly), a home for the aged, day-care facilities for children, 130 rooms for youths aged eighteen to twenty-five, and 49 rooms for "youth pensions," for young people between the ages of fourteen and eighteen. Here, too, the accommodations are scattered around the complex. One pattern followed here is placing several rooms around each staircase connecting the floors of a five-story building. Each two rooms share a bathroom and there is a common cafeteria and kitchen where meals are provided.

Twenty-two-year-old Preben is typical of a second large category of youths who live in these facilities—those who come from rural areas far

from Copenhagen, have no family nearby, and find difficulty in adapt-
ing to the pressures and complexities of urban life. After Preben arrived
in the city, he found a job, but was scrounging for a place to live, staying a few weeks in a sort of "hippie" commune, then in another, unable
to find any decent, cheap place of his own. He was depressed, caught
up with an unstable group of youths, and on the verge of losing his
job. A fellow worker told him of Ungbo; he applied, was interviewed
and accepted. Although he considers this a temporary arrangement until
he can earn more money, he is quite enthusiastic about his room and,
for the first time in six months, has begun to make friends and to plan
for the future.

Finally, the dens are designed to meet the needs of a third group of
youths, and to serve another function: to provide a protected environment and opportunity for socialization for maladjusted youths or youths
with physical, mental, emotional, or cultural handicaps. (An illustration of the last are young people coming from Greenland, who have
major problems in adjusting to a radically different sociocultural environment.) In order to facilitate the adjustment and socialization of
these youths, up to 15 percent of the rooms in each den division are
reserved for them. No more than this percentage is allocated for these
"restricted" categories, because the objective is to integrate them into
the populaton of "normal" or "average" youths—apprentices, workers,
vocational students—who have only "ordinary" problems.

For the same reason as in France, university students are generally
excluded from these accommodations. Similarly, youths who have completed higher education and are financially and otherwise able to obtain
adequate housing on their own are excluded. The assumption is that
this housing is for those who need it most—for economic, social, or
psychological reasons.

In contrast to the dens, which offer relatively independent living
arrangements for youths aged eighteen to twenty-five, the "children and
youth pensions" provide a more protected environment for youngsters
under the age of eighteen. The "children's pensions" are for those under
fourteen and are designed to take in children for a very brief period,
generally not more than three months. They provide closely supervised
accommodations for a small number, most of whom are children of
residents temporarily unable to care for them because of illness or hospitalization. The youth pensions are for fourteen to eighteen year olds,
especially sixteen to eighteen, and although more extensive than the
children's pensions, are far fewer in number than the dens. The total
number of young people in these pensions is about five hundred. There

are twelve youth pensions and eight integrated children's and youth pensions in twenty housing projects. As an illustration of how extensive these facilities are, in one project there are 49 single rooms, with 250 dens and 2,000 apartments for families. The pensions tend to be clustered more closely together and are far more closely supervised, frequently with one resident social worker for every five or six youngsters. Although the average stay is between six months and one year, two groups of youths predominate here: the first are those who stay for a brief period of time—a few weeks or at most a few months. These are "ordinary" teenagers who need temporary care away from home because a parent is ill or because there is some temporary, short-term crisis at home, or even because parents are away for a few weeks on vacation and do not want the youngsters to stay alone. The second group is composed of children requiring more extended care, perhaps two or three years, and often having more severe problems. These may be children from broken homes where neither parent can care for the youngsters, or children who have been cared for by a grandparent who is now ill and unable to cope with the needs and demands of a teenager, or children whose behavior at home or in school has led to conflict with the authorities and a subsequent recommendation by the court that the child be placed in a supervised and protected environment. Finally, there is a third group of youngsters in these facilities, those who have been institutionalized, either for reasons of delinquency or mental illness, for whom these pensions provide a kind of halfway house.

Annaliese, a sixteen-year-old girl, lives in one of five rooms surrounding a central stairwell in one such facility. There are two other floors above with similar accommodations, a common living room, and a cafeteria where all meals are taken. Annaliese's mother died last year and her father's work involves frequent travel. She was often left alone and began truanting from school. When a teacher suggested this facility to her father, he eagerly followed up on it. Annaliese has now been living in the pension for two months. A social worker lives on the same floor and is assigned to the three girls and two boys on the floor. She arranges group activities and also spends time with each youngster on an individual basis. Annaliese assumes that in another year, when she is old enough, she will move into one of the dens in the project.

Another approach to housing these teenagers is still in the experimental stage. It involves scattering accommodations for those under eighteen among the dens for the older youth, just as the dens are scattered in small groups among family apartments. Fairly close supervision would continue to be provided; however, an implicit assumption is that the older youths would provide role models for the younger ones, and thus less formal supervision would be required. Once again, this is all part of the Danish philosophy of integrating all age groups and maintaining as normal a living environment as possible regardless of special needs.

Although staff have had only limited formal training, the social workers have all had extensive direct, practical experience in working with youths, are young themselves, and relate easily to the residents. They understand their problems and are committed to helping them. There have been problems with drug use and abuse in the past but these have decreased in recent years. However, in part the decrease in drug abuse has been offset by an increase in problems of alcohol abuse. It is of some concern to the administration.

In a context of widespread social acceptance, sexual activity is rarely described as a problem. Pregnancy occurs infrequently because contraceptive devices as well as information and counseling are readily available. If a girl does become pregnant, an abortion can be performed legally; if the girl wishes to keep her child, no opprobrium is attached and she is helped to obtain other accommodations, often elsewhere in the same housing development, since it is considered important that she not be isolated from friends and other known supports.

In general, when the young people are ready to move out, they are helped to find housing elsewhere. It is assumed that changing living arrangements is all part of the normal process of moving from dependency to semi-independence and finally to completely independent living. The Danes are continually exploring, testing, and revising various approaches to meeting the special needs of these youths.

Although almost every one of the more than twenty-five such housing developments that have such facilities for youths has its own style of operation and provision, all support one common theme: promoting the socialization, development, and well-being of youth in its transition to adulthood. Recognizing the growing numbers of youth needing or wanting to live alone, the Danes understand that at the same time that the period of schooling for young people—and therefore school-leaving ages—has been extended, physical maturity and the desire for independence and freedom are occurring at an earlier age. The need to be dependent on parents for financial support and the desire for independence in social behavior have caused increased parent-adolescent conflict over an extended period of time. These dens and youth pensions represent one approach to resolving this conflict. Furthermore, recognizing the necessity for alternative forms of away-from-home care for young people with problems, the facilities represent an effort at satisfying these needs also. For all youths, those with problems and those without, the Danish philosophy is that it is best to provide opportunities for socialization, maturation, and increased independence in a context in which youths are living close to their families and in a normal environment.

We in the United States have a limited and declining network of YMCA's and YWCA's and—for troubled youth—halfway houses and urban treatment homes. The more affluent, as noted, are catered to in the marketplace. The others—*most* young people—are on their own, despite evidence that this is not good enough. Americans clearly do not like the results, but have not yet invested in improvement.

5

Helping People at Home

in Sweden and the Netherlands

MRS. M. has been hospitalized suddenly. Her husband is unable to take time off from work to take care of the children, and there is no relative or neighbor to care for the baby or help with cooking, cleaning, shopping, and other household chores.

Johnny is home from first grade because of a sore throat. His mother works and has no one to stay with him.

The old man in the apartment upstairs feels helpless after the sudden death of his wife. He cannot cope with the housework and needs someone to help him bathe and take him for a walk.

Seventy-three-year-old Mrs. L. is frightened about living alone after having had a heart attack. She worries about carrying heavy packages from the supermarket, and she cannot do the laundry or the heavy cleaning.

In Sweden, home helps—publicly employed and paid and specially trained—can provide assistance in such cases. All that is needed is a telephone call to the local municipal Home Help Service, where the "organizer" in charge of social services for the neighborhood will obtain the facts, assess the need for help, and make appropriate arrangements. Services are available, on request, to people of all classes and income levels. Although wealthy people may purchase such services elsewhere, middle-class, working-class, and poor people make regular and frequent use of a range of services provided under this program. Services are free to the poor and are paid for by others according to a sliding scale of fees related to the income of the recipient. "Light" medical or nursing care is provided free to all.

The Netherlands, another high-coverage country, follows a somewhat different administrative pattern. Public funds are channeled through many private nonprofit groups, which actually deliver this service. Here, too, home helps are valued highly and are considered essential to a modern society.

Home Help in Sweden

Observing a home help organizer at work on an average day and asking her questions give some idea of the services; what home help workers are like; how they are selected and trained; whom they help and what they do; how extensive the service is and what some of the problems are.

Mrs. O. is a typical home help organizer. Trained as a social worker (some are trained as nurses), she is currently employed by the Stockholm Municipal Home Help Service Agency in a branch office located in a large suburban housing development. She is one of a staff of twelve who are responsible for the supervision of 467 home helps, working from two to twenty-five hours per week (although more and more home helps are working a full forty-hour week), servicing 1,069 old people. This concentration on older people is quite routine in Sweden today; about three-quarters of the services provided go to either the elderly or the handicapped, while only about one-quarter are directed toward families with young children.

Mrs. O. supervises and organizes the work of thirty-seven home helps, who in turn provide a range of services and care to the 137 elderly people composing her caseload. The morning we visited began, as she explained, like every other morning, with a three-hour "telephone time" from 8:00 to 11:00 A.M. People call with requests for service, for information, to change appointments, to complain. Home help staff call to obtain their instructions for the day, to offer information based on the previous day's experiences, or to notify the organizer of their illness and the need for a replacement to be sent out. Some staff come directly to the office, but most report by telephone because the community is large and spread out and traveling to the office is time-consuming.

During these hours Mrs. O. also has to schedule future jobs as requests for service arise, arrange substitutes for part-time staff unable to work that day, and respond to questions and complaints. She called one elderly man to notify him of a change in schedule. She called another to prepare him for the fact that his regular worker was ill, and a "stranger" would come that day to bathe him and cook him a meal. Following a call from another "customer," she phoned a woman's regular home help to ask her to accompany the woman to a doctor's appointment, wait for her, and then take her home.

A staff member called in sick and Mrs. O. phoned each of her clients to ask if they could manage without help for a day or two. She explained to us that if they can take care of themselves and just need help for cleaning or occasional chores, they will wait until their "regular" is back. But older people who need personal care and cooking services cannot wait and Mrs. O. arranged for substitute helpers to be sent them. In cases such as these, or other emergencies where a client becomes ill and suddenly requires help, it may be necessary to reschedule a worker's time, temporarily eliminating service to a more independent older person in order to provide care for the more needy; but no such change is made without notifying the client.

An eighty-two-year-old man called to request thorough cleaning for his apartment. Mrs. O. tried to arrange for this from the municipal service patrol—a specially equipped truck with trained personnel who do heavy cleaning for the elderly and/or handicapped—but their schedule was very busy and they could not service him for several months. She called him back and suggested waiting for the service, but he was insistent, becoming increasingly upset at the idea of a delay. His daughter was coming to visit him for the first time in a long while, and he wanted his home to be spotless when she saw it. Mrs. O. tried again, unsuccessfully, to obtain service from a private cleaning firm. Finally, she remembered that a home help in one of the other districts "specializes" in heavy cleaning, because she enjoys it. Mrs. O. called the organizer in that district, and they worked out an arrangement for an exchange of services.

Later on in the morning Mrs. O. was faced with the unpleasant task of having to discharge one of her staff. The woman had been late, repeatedly, in arriving for her scheduled appointments and on several occasions had neither shown up nor telephoned. Even worse, she had been indiscreet, repeating a confidence given by one of her elderly pensioners. Mrs. O. explained to us that working with the elderly requires patience, sensitivity, warmth, and tact. Indeed, her manner on the telephone, with both her own staff and her clients, is a remarkable illustration of all these qualities.

After lunch, we accompanied Mrs. O. as she made home visits. Every "customer" is visited at least once during the time service is provided, and more often if there is regular, ongoing care involved. In addition, special visits are made if there are problems, or if the case is a "difficult" one. Our first visit was to the home of Mrs. T., a seventy-eight-year-old woman who had been living alone since her husband died a few months before. She was afraid to open her door when we arrived, and only after several minutes of reassurance by Mrs. O. did she unbolt it, first checking our appearance through the half-open chained door. Mrs. O. talked with her briefly, asking her if she was satisfied with her helper. Had the marketing been done properly? Was the house cleaned well? Was everything all right? Mrs. T. complained about the service, but was so vague that it was hard to tell what the problem was. After some probing by Mrs. O., it appeared that Mrs. T. was becoming increasingly frightened about going out alone in the street, and even about being home alone. She has no relatives or friends, and what she fears most is becoming ill with no one knowing. Mrs. O. tried to reassure her, suggesting that she schedule a helper to come in three times weekly, for slightly shorter periods of time, instead of the twice-a-week service Mrs. T. was then receiving. As we left, Mrs. O. mentioned to us the need for a more extensive telephone visiting service for the isolated elderly like Mrs. T.

Our second visit was to seventy-three-year-old Mr. Z., living alone since his wife died. He immediately initiated a discussion of his finances, explaining that his wife had always handled household expenses and he was having difficulty managing food purchases because prices were so high. Mrs. O. spent some time helping him prepare a weekly budget. Apart from having someone come in once a week to clean and do laundry, Mr. Z. is totally independent.

We stopped next at Mrs. Q.'s because she had been to the doctor's the day before and her helper had reported to Mrs. O. that she thinks more regular service is needed. Mrs. O. wanted to see how Mrs. Q. felt, suggest more extensive service, but review first with Mrs. Q. what additional kinds of help she thought she needed and how best to schedule service.

Our fourth visit was to a seventy-six-year-old woman who was entering the hospital shortly for an operation. Her eighty-year-old husband is severely arthritic and she was concerned about leaving him alone. Our visit here was extensive, as Mrs. O. reviewed with the woman her husband's needs and wants, and what the best plan might be for helping him while she was hospitalized—and helping both of them on her return home, while she convalesced.

Our last visit of the day was to Mrs. R., also to discuss her financial situation. She is a mildly senile woman, very absent-minded and forgetful. She could not remember where she put her bank books, and had no money for food. The helper had called Mrs. O. earlier, to report the loss. Apparently this is a frequent occurrence and after searching in several places—in a drawer among her underclothes, in back of the sugar bowl, on a top shelf in the closet—Mrs. O. wearily promised to call Mrs. R.'s daughter and ask her to try to locate the bank books or have them replaced. Mrs. O. told us that this happens several times a month, but usually Mrs. R. remembers in a day or so where she put them, only to forget again later. Mrs. R. is so forgetful that she sometimes fails to eat the meal prepared for her by the home help and on other occasions eats the meal but insists she hasn't and says none was ever prepared. Mrs. O. and the helper, in case of emergency, keep in touch with the daughter, who lives some distance away. They have all agreed that as long as it is possible they will help Mrs. R. stay in her own home, since she becomes distraught at any suggestion of leaving it. Mrs. O.'s last action before starting for her own home was to make a note to call Mrs. R.'s daughter during her telephone time the next morning. And so her day ends.

Although almost all the western European countries have much more extensive home help service than we do in the United States, Sweden's publicly funded, organized, and delivered system of services for the elderly, the handicapped, or families with children in need of temporary help is particularly well developed. In fact, more than 1 percent (87,000) of Sweden's eight million inhabitants work as home helps, employed full time or part time, by the hour or by the day, providing different types of care and exposed to different levels of training. Granted that less than four thousand of these are full-time workers, and another eighteen thousand are part of Sweden's unique program whereby relatives may be paid for caring for family members under special circumstances, this still represents the equivalent of approximately one full-time worker for every 260 people.

There are three major categories of home help service in Sweden:

Domestic helpers are homemakers or "housewife substitutes," specially trained women who serve as housekeepers or surrogate mothers, assisting families with children when the mother is not able to manage her home because of a serious illness or hospitalization. This type of assistance can also be given to a housewife in need of help to prevent illness or overstrain. It is essentially temporary or short-term emergency help.

Home care attendants are women who provide regular and continuing assistance to the aged and handicapped. This service usually involves light nursing care, personal care, and a range of household and chore services, and is expected to be ongoing and long term.

Child care attendants provide temporary child care when a child in a day nursery or primary school is ill or in need of someone to care for him at home.

Modeled after a similar program in Britain, home help service was first introduced in Sweden by the Swedish Red Cross during the 1920s. The program continued under the auspices of this and other voluntary organizations until the 1940s, when the government began to assume responsibility for service provision. Initially, the program was directed primarily toward provision of emergency services to families with small children when the mother was ill or unable for some other reason to cope with household responsibilities and child care. At first, these consisted of routine housekeeping chores in addition to some personal care (e.g., bathing a sick person). Gradually, the service was expanded to include shopping, escort, information, and referral services. Coverage has increased enormously during the last decade and since 1965 has been provided by the local municipalities and funded by the central government on a 35/65 matching basis. (It is anticipated that this will soon be changed to a 50/50 basis.)

At the beginning, the service was provided solely by middle-aged women whose children were grown and whose household responsibilities had decreased, leaving them with spare time (but limited skills) to do some kind of work. Part-time employment in managing other households seemed a natural and convenient form of work for people already experienced in running a house. Usually working only a few hours a week, these women received little or no training and had no trade union affiliation and no social security rights. The first qualified, regular home helps underwent special training programs for eight months at first and then for up to eighteen months, including child-care practice, domestic work, and training in light medical or nursing care. As the service expanded, training became more formalized and consistent, but also shorter and more specialized, related directly to the type of service to be provided. Even today, some inconsistency persists between, for example, Stockholm and the rest of the country. Most home helps outside Stockholm are required to undergo a 160-hour training program that includes courses in psychology, child development, nutrition and home economics, labor market questions, sociology, and health care. Practical experience is also required in traditional household chores. In contrast, home helps in Stockholm go through an intensive one-week training program only, providing general information on services for the elderly, food suitable for the elderly, light medical and personal care, shopping, and the like. In addition, for workers who will be caring for the more "difficult" cases (handicapped or mentally ill), there are additional required courses, among them special courses for care of the sick (24 hours), for care of the mentally ill (24 hours), for care of those with impaired hearing (20 hours), for care of the blind

(20 hours), and on nutrition (12 hours). Workers receive their regular salary while they are being trained. For home care attendants providing "night-watching" in homes of the sick or frail elderly, two special courses of forty-two lessons each are provided under the auspices of the Red Cross. (All other training is done under governmental auspices.) These courses are compulsory for all doing this type of work unless they have had previous nursing training or extensive experience, and workers do not receive salaries while in this program. Throughout the service, in Stockholm and the rest of Sweden, the home help service organizers have much more training than the workers themselves; they generally are either social workers or nurses, and one current complaint by staff is the built-in dichotomy between supervisors and the home helps.

Although the service was initiated primarily for families with children, by the late 1950s, as a result of declining birth rates and increased longevity, the quantity of care had increased and the focus of the program changed to include greater stress on service for the elderly and the handicapped. At the same time two other types of service emerged: home-care attendants, specially trained and more experienced workers, akin to social workers, who work with the more complicated and demanding cases (usually the mentally ill or more severely handicapped); and child-care attendants, who take care of children of working or studying parents when the child is ill and cannot attend his usual day-care center or school. Currently, these workers are also used to substitute for family day-care mothers in case of their illness, or temporarily to replace staff in day-care centers or nursery schools when needed.

As demand for service grew, various innovative approaches to provision were developed. For example, in sparsely populated areas where home helps are scarce, mobile service teams operate. In addition, where there is extensive demand for specialized services such as heavy cleaning for elderly or handicapped people living alone, similar mobile services have been developed. Stockholm initiated "service vans" in the mid-1960s—two-member working teams who carry with them special equipment and specialize in miscellaneous heavy cleaning jobs such as washing windows and floors, waxing floors, and so forth. In the countryside, such special mobile teams may also have equipment for hairdressing, meals-on-wheels, home delivery of frozen and other foods, arrangements for carrying books back and forth from the public library to the isolated and homebound.

The newest "home help" is the rural mailman (or woman). By an agreement between the postal service and the local social welfare organizations, the rural mailman is subsidized for taking over some social services—for instance, to check up on the condition of an elderly person living alone, help him or her to chop wood, bring in water, or clear snow, contact a doctor or social worker, shop, bring food and medicine, or just visit and provide a little companionship. The postal service charges 88¢ for each errand. The recipient pays half the cost of this service if he can afford it; otherwise, it is free, paid for by local government.

As noted earlier, home help services are available to all people (and used by almost all) regardless of income level. Light medical or nursing care (chiropodist services; bathing the elderly or ill person; helping a patient take medication; treating bed sores; taking temperature and pulse) is provided free of charge to all. However, other services are paid for according to income, on a sliding scale. Thus, an old person who pays for domestic help is charged a maximum of $2.64 per hour (a fee that does not cover the actual cost of service) and about one-fifth of those receiving services pay this fee; most pay nothing. One of the most important aspects of the service for the elderly is that help can be obtained as it is needed, for only one or two hours a day, once or twice a week. (Of course, more extensive service is available if needed and wanted.) This means that old people do not have to commit themselves to a whole day of service, when what they really need is several brief periods of care each week. At present, the government is spending about $60.5 million for home help services, and planned expenditures for 1974–75 are $66 million. About the same amount is spent by local government. And about 10 percent of the central government expenditures is for experimental programs for providing care for the elderly and handicapped in sparsely populated areas.

Of the 8,000,000 people living in Sweden, more than 1,300,000 are over sixty-seven (the retirement age in Sweden), and more than one-tenth of these receive some form of home help service. In general, more services are provided in the large cities such as Stockholm or Göteborg, because more old people live there and, for a variety of reasons, they tend to stay out of institutions until they are well into their eighties. If one looks at the overall volume of home help service, most goes for the care of the elderly and handicapped. Yet of the approximately 1,000,000 Swedes who are members of families with young children, 10 percent also received some form of home help service (as of the late

1960s); more than one-half of these received domestic help (the emergency, short-term home help service) while the remainder utilized the temporary child-care service.

A few of the homemakers still work for voluntary organizations but the overwhelming percentage of service is provided by the government directly under local public auspices. Fully trained personnel employed by municipalities are paid $550 a month for a full-time job (about 37.5 hours per week, but the exact amount may vary from week to week). If they remain overnight in a home (but are not working as "night watchers"), they receive a small additional supplement. Home-care attendants and child-care attendants are usually employed on a part-time basis and are paid about $3.00 an hour, the equivalent of what an unskilled industrial worker earns. Supplementary wages are paid to those who work odd shifts (evenings or weekends). Only a small percentage of these workers are unionized although by now all are covered by social security benefits. This lack of unionization and of organization tends to underscore the low status of the job and the weakness of the bargaining position of these women.

As the demand for service continues to grow at an increasingly rapid rate, there is great concern in Sweden that the quality of service has not kept pace with expanded quantity. *Women in Municipal Service*, a recent report of a special Task Force for Women appointed by the municipal (city) council of Stockholm, is very critical of the home help program in Stockholm. The report concludes that the service is provided almost exclusively by women, the work is clearly of low status, workers have little job security (since most are part-time), and working conditions are unsatisfactory (for example, an elderly client may see no need to have a good reading lamp available for a "night watcher"). Many are employed and paid by the hour and cannot plan how extensively they will work from week to week. They receive little training (only one-fifth have taken the longer 160-hour training program required elsewhere in Sweden), work without contact with other colleagues, and have few opportunities for promotion or career advancement. The Task Force made certain recommendations to the Stockholm social welfare administration. Among these are the following: (1) the number of home-care attendants (those serving the handicapped and the elderly) should be substantially increased; (2) special efforts should be made to recruit men for the service, beginning with a few pilot programs in one or two districts; (3) basic training should be extended to cover the standard 160-hour program instituted elsewhere in Sweden; (4) additional, more specialized and advanced training programs should be developed (and workers paid salaries while in these programs); (5) training programs and career ladders should be developed whereby home helps might be able to become home help organizers; and (6) efforts should be made to institute group meetings among the home helps as well as other approaches to increase their contact with one another. In addition, home helps should be encouraged to participate more actively in the organization and management of their work.

One home help commenting about the need for more and improved training said, "Although most home helps are experienced housewives—women over forty who have been married and raised families of their own—it is important for young girls to come into the service too. What is really needed is a good, basic introductory training course for girls who have never managed their own homes. They don't need courses in cleaning with complicated machines, the way they teach the course now. An old person often has only one room and a tiny kitchen and you don't need any special equipment to clean that. And they don't need to learn so much theory. What these girls really need to learn is how to listen patiently to old people. Ninety percent of our job consists of just listening. And another piece is getting the old ones to go outside for a walk, even if just for a little while. The cleaning part is the least important; often it's the company and a little attention that makes the real difference."

Home Help in the Netherlands

The Netherlands warrants discussion both because of its substantial coverage and because of its use of private, charity-based agencies to deliver home help service. In this sense—public reimbursement but decentralized, voluntary agency–based administration—the Dutch pattern will be familiar to Americans.

The Netherlands is working actively to decrease its institutionalized population of the aged and to cut the future ratio of institutionalized care. Another motive for expanding the home help service, although of lesser importance, is the desire to avoid family breakup in emergencies. It is estimated that in 1973 the Netherlands had a staff of some 55,000 women carrying out home help activities. About 14,000–15,000 actually work at the job full time and tend to be assigned to family situations in which the mother cannot fulfill her responsibilities because of a family emergency or a personal disability. These full-time workers tend to include the 7,000 formally trained home helps. The others, some 45,000

older women, work about one-third time, at hours which both suit
their own situations and meet the needs for service. These are married
people or widows who want to do part-time work. Life experience,
rather than school, prepares them. In addition, there are administrative
and "support" personnel.

As is true of many social services in Europe, the home help expansion occurred after World War II. Budgetary appropriations by government for this purpose have increased dramatically, and by 1972 total
expenditures were $123.5 million, with the government paying $98.8
million. Thus, government meets more than four-fifths of the total cost,
and the difference is made up by user fees and private charitable contributions.

The Netherlands Homemaker Service was developed and is administered by several hundred voluntary independent agencies which are
subsidized by the central government. In recent years, public policy has
encouraged agencies to merge their operations through consolidation or
affiliation in order to effect economies of scale. Larger agencies are able
to support a more extensive range of services and to provide professional supervision. Closer ties with social work practice and connection
with other social services are also facilitated.

Americans may find this pattern interesting, given our limited development thus far and our considerable commitment to the voluntary
sector. The Dutch have been proud of their ability to use administrative
and financial incentives to reduce the agencies rendering service from
about one thousand to under five hundred. Their recent administrative
research documents as an achievement the gradual growth since 1968
in agency case loads and staffs and the modest tendency to move from
a completely sectarian voluntary pattern of organization to a system
with more nonsectarian services. There are still six major national voluntary organizations in the field, but they are coordinated by a national
central agency. Increased centralization is being sought even as government increases its own leadership role.

But how does the service operate? Application for service may be
made directly to the agency either by telephone (as in Amsterdam) or
in person at the agency offices (as in Arnhem). As in the Swedish program, after basic particulars are taken regarding the family situation, a
home visit is arranged to round out the information necessary for assessment of the client's need for service and to determine the kind of help
that should be offered, the amount of time required of the worker, and
so forth. Two to four hours one to three times a week is common for
the aged. Family emergencies require full-time coverage. The fee—ap-

proximately $29 a week at the time of our visits, well beyond the ability of the average person to pay completely—is met in part by government subsidy and in part by an income-related weekly payment. If the applicant cannot meet his part of the agency's fees, an application for subsidy is made in his behalf to the local public assistance authorities which provide social aid to those in need. In Amsterdam the local authority, by gentlemen's agreement, accepts the agency's determination of financial ability to pay, making it unnecessary for the client to approach the local authority himself, a procedure designed to minimize embarrassment. Thus we find an approach similar to that used in Sweden: a universal service with a sliding fee scale based on financial ability as assessed by the agency in discussion with the client, and coverage on a "means test" basis for those who can pay no fee at all. Assignment of the case to a home help worker for service is made through the "leader" or "guide," as first-level supervisors are called; these may or may not be social workers. Supervisory direction of the leaders is exercised by a chief social worker. Such a three-tier organizational structure also accommodates specialist workers and, in the case of broad-purpose agencies, provides for liaison with other service sectors of the agency.

The government controls expenditures by means of subsidy regulations and a budget. Each voluntary agency is given a ceiling quota for reimbursement upon which it draws (at an agreed rate per service unit) as it renders services. A computer program produces a monthly balance for each agency. A small reserve fund and a shifting of funds at the year's end take care of overspending. (This approach to management is part of the force behind the effort to consolidate small programs.)

Line personnel in the homemaker service consist of on-the-job or briefly trained part-time home helps; full-time home helps, who may receive training of up to a year; and professionally trained homemakers. The latter are graduates of a training school. Although they are described as "professionals," we would not consider them such; European usage of the word "professional" seems to correspond to our use of "occupational" or "vocational." Although staff are almost exclusively women, the Netherlands, like Sweden and Britain, is attempting to recruit men into the service, so far with very limited success.

The geriatric service is staffed by the part-time workers, recruited from the ranks of lower-middle-class and working-class housewives who provide well-defined domiciliary help that enables old people to live in their own homes, thereby postponing or avoiding institutionalization. Services include cleaning, food preparation, shopping, personal help, bathing, and dressing. This is not a medical care service; if a nurse is needed, one is called. However, help with dressing, and what the Swedish term "light medical care," is in order.

Home helps in geriatric service are minimally trained on the job; as experienced housewives, they are seen as ready for the household demands of the job, although they receive some guidance through their leaders (supervisors) to enable them to spot cases which should be referred for additional attention or for special help or more frequent visits. They are expected to watch for changes in health status, nutritional practice, physical activity. Sometimes volunteers are available for household repair work, for taking clients for walks, for errands, or for sewing. A large home help agency would not ordinarily organize such voluntary services, leaving that task to other community organizations (churches, for example), but when such help for the aged is available it is used by the home help agency as an additional resource that supplements or substitutes for the basic service. One agency regarded such volunteer work as a useful supplement, but another expressed some reservations about its regular reliability. As noted, part-time workers are employed to provide home help to old people, and for the foreseeable future, recruitment of personnel is expected to be adequate.

The general family service is staffed by professionally trained home helps who, as their title suggests, perform substitute household-management and child-care tasks for a housewife in the event of her illness, absence, incapacity, or incompetence. The service is based on the belief that providing a substitute for the housewife is often necessary, but it is emphasized that the home help is not a member of the family and that maintaining "professional distance" is appropriate. Although she may help out over a prolonged period, round-the-clock services, for example, are not provided, and only in an extreme emergency may she stay with a family overnight, and then only with the supervisor's permission and with provision made for appropriate overtime payment, time off, and so forth. This policy is intended in part to prevent the possibility of exploitation and in the interest of regularizing hours of work and other aspects of the job.

The services of professionally trained home helps, or school graduates, are ordinarily reserved for difficult cases such as may be presented by a family which is large, has several young children, or includes a handicapped member. Some school graduates with experience may take additional training to become specialists, working with problem families, overburdened mothers, the chronically ill, the mentally disturbed, the retarded, and so forth. The home help's task is to perform a working, helping, or teaching role as required by the family after assessment of circumstances and need. In general, emphasis is placed on the concrete nature of the service and on meeting the specific needs of the client. When assigned to a case, the worker receives instructions from the leader regarding management of the case. After supervisory discussion of an ongoing case, the worker may be given special tasks related to a treatment objective—for example, to teach a mother how to play with a child, to encourage independence, or to avoid overdependence.

Professional home help is time-limited. A six-month assignment to a case would be the outside limit and exceptional. It is agency policy to help the family make alternative arrangements to meet continuing requirements through relatives, through reorganization of household management, or through the market. Responsibility to help the family work out such arrangements would lie with the leader or possibly, in a large agency, with another staff member.

Something of the flavor of the service is suggested by looking at the training program for homemakers. The training school we visited in Arnhem, like the others (about twenty-five in all), is privately run and directed. Curriculum is influenced by government policy as expressed through the Education Ministry and through the family affairs division of the Ministry of Culture, Recreation, and Social Work. Also involved, of course, is the national organization, the Central Board of Home Help Service in the Netherlands. The students, a young, lively, attractive group, look much like American high school seniors or college freshmen. Living quarters are in an old mansion of some elegance, set in a garden. Most of the ground floor is taken up by a spacious living or common room, very tastefully furnished and decorated. The bedrooms, upstairs, were somewhat simpler in decor but pleasant and also furnished in good taste, with two, three, or four students to a room, depending on its size.

The school currently draws most of its students from young women who have been employed by home help agencies for six months and who have been selected to be sent for training, with expenses paid by the agency in return for a commitment to return to employment after graduation. Applications for admission must also be supported by recommendations from the home-town school and from other sources, as well as a home visit with the applicant's family. The training course has a duration of one-and-a-half years; the first six months are spent in residence, since this is predominantly the period of classroom and theoretical studies although supervised fieldwork is also gradually introduced. The curriculum is organized in units, emphasizing such areas as religious and cultural influences on family life and development; primary social units and social structures; the housewife's role and child rearing; and the homemaker function. Practical laboratory work starts in the school, accompanied in the first eight weeks of the course by a half-day per week spent in the field under the supervision of "a good house-wife" who functions as a field instructor. Thereafter, the student moves to somewhat longer and more difficult field placements with regular normal-client families assigned through the home help agency, and even-tually to some experience with more complex problems (for example, a family with a member with a mild handicap). Case experiences are writ-ten up by the student and used for class discussion.

Across the road from the school's residential quarters is another building housing "laboratories" and ordinary classrooms. Here are laundry rooms with various washing and pressing machines, kitchens with a range of appliances and cookers, cleaning aids of different types, all apparently designed to familiarize students with the types of equip-ment that they may expect to encounter in practice. Indeed, the equip-ment is so varied, shiny, and elegant that one is prompted to wonder if the girls would be ready to adapt to and cope with households that are less generously equipped.

At the beginning of the course the student is introduced to social structures by being sent out to interview a variety of people—police and post office officials, staffs of social and welfare agencies, old people at home. Educational experiences are faithfully recorded in a log—an edu-cational scrapbook, or record—together with special essays, observa-tions, newspaper clippings, and photographs to illustrate ranges of hu-man emotions, evaluations, recommendations. The book provides a complete record of the student's educational experience.

After six months of residence, marked by continuous evaluation by everyone with whom the student is educationally involved, there is a final examination to conclude the first phase of the course, with exam-ination questions covering materials studied on family structure, social agencies, social insurance, and homemaker theory, and including a case analysis. Among materials submitted for final evaluation is the student's profile of a family, with attention to strengths and problems.

After she completes the six months of academic work in residence, the student returns to the agency for a "block placement"—a year's su-pervised work, starting with simple case assignments and moving to work with families of large size, problem situations, and the like. Again, records are kept for fortnightly supervisory evaluation. During the practice year students return to the school for five study days—discus-sion, special lectures, and so forth.

This is an occupation, not a "profession" in the usual sense of the term. As in Sweden, administration and supervision are usually assigned to social workers, nurses, public administration personnel—not to experienced home help graduates.

The home help service is widely used, predominantly by working- and middle-class families; the well-to-do tend to make private arrangements. Informants expressed some amusement when asked if any attempt is made to publicize the service, and then suggested that recruitment publicity serves to make the service known. In any case, the emergence of large professionally staffed agencies providing other social services as well (see below) brings home help resources into direct contact with potential clients. Despite widespread knowledge of the service, however, some doctors apparently are not familiar with it. And there are also some misconceptions; sometimes households will seek home helps for the "spring cleaning."

An Underdeveloped Service in the United States

In the United States the home help is referred to by a number of names— "homemaker," "home health aide," "home aide"—but the description officially adopted by the national standard-setting organization and increasingly used by local agencies is "homemaker–home health aide." Whatever the names—or the reasons—this is a service field in which we lag.[1] According to a 1972 report to a U.S. Senate subcommittee on aging, the international association in the homemaker field suggested that there is reasonable coverage when a country has one homemaker per 1,500 population. The American rate is one per 7,000, with a heavy clustering on the eastern seaboard. France has one per 2,000; Denmark one per 760; the United Kingdom one per 667; and the Netherlands one per 380. In general most of these personnel serve the elderly. In Britain, the rate is 5.5 home helps per 1,000 elderly, and the government sees the need for a twofold or threefold expansion.[2]

Norms are not firmly established in this field but experience suggests that at least 15 percent of the elderly can make good use of the service. The demand for family services will vary with many social fac-

1. For recent U.S. data write to the National Council for Homemaker–Home Health Aide Services, 67 Irving Place, New York City, 10003.
2. In 1972 there were 2,600 full-time homemakers or home helps in the U.K. and 72,000 part-timers. The full-time equivalent total was 35,185. The coverage was 15 per 10,000 population, while the Dutch rate was over 26.

tors in a given place. If the United States were to match the Dutch coverage rate we would have 400,000 to 500,000. If we were to meet the
recommendation of the International Association our total would be
about 150,000. The White House Conference on Aging saw need for
300,000. Our current total is closer to 40,000.

The service in the United States, like that in Sweden, began as a way
of allowing children to stay in their own homes during emergency absences of their parents, but has increasingly been used for the elderly
and handicapped. The homemaker–home health aide service is posi-
tively regarded, by those who understand it, as a preventive child welfare
service.

It is widely believed and has been occasionally shown that in-home
services can be provided with less cost, in both money and human
stress, than out-of-home care. It has been repeatedly shown that "emergency" use of out-of-home care is likely to lead to long-term care or
permanent family breakup.

Strangely, despite this, the need for homemaker service as a family
and child welfare preventive measure has led to only modest provision
everywhere—few metropolitan areas in the United States have significant coverage. Despite the relative frequency of family emergencies and
the needs of families who are often far from relatives and friends who
might help out, the burden remains on the individual family. People find
their own resources and pay for the service out of their own pockets.
The homemaker working in families with children becomes a symbol
of dependency, neglect, poverty, disorganization—and her assistance is
not seen as a necessity similar to medical and nursing care. And as is
often the case, because average people do not identify with such needs,
provision remains inadequate. After all, it is for "those others."

On the other hand, the obvious need of older people for help to
make it possible for them to continue an independent life in the community, instead of having to rely on institutional care, has apparently
spurred a substantial expansion in services in the United States, as in
much of Europe. The expansion continues as the aged constitute increasingly significant percentages of the total population—not that we
in the United States have followed this to any logical conclusion. Home
health aides in the United States are available for up to one hundred
days of service through Medicare, but only by referral of a physician,
after at least three days of hospitalization or nursing home care, not as
a preventive service. Little service is available; and for what there is
available, on a fee-for-service basis, costs are prohibitive to most individuals—about $4.50 per hour—far beyond what the average older

person can afford.[3] Homemaker services also have been funded out of the Older Americans Act, but only on a project basis and on a declining scale. Most of the remainder of the public funding is as a public welfare social service, requiring a diagnostic assessment and the economic status designated as the eligibility level in each state. Government has concentrated on payment, not on service delivery, and our development is on quite a small scale compared with that of European leaders. Voluntary philanthropy seems to favor homemaker–home health aides, but the resources from this source are limited. Expansion of in-home services was urged by the most recent White House Conference on Aging.

In short, we should recognize the need for two types of service: homemaker–home health aide service in conjunction with professional therapy and a more routine service to meet common, widely shared needs for supplementary household service and help. The latter category justifies large-scale coverage lest old people in particular find that they cannot remain in the community. Both the Netherlands and Sweden, as well as Britain, Denmark, France, and West Germany among other European countries, recognize the need for large-scale staffing. The United States does not; or at least our performance suggests that we do not, despite rhetorical statements to the contrary.

There are, of course, issues and debates among the Europeans. The development of the service away from a narrowly "domestic work" function (housework, not individualized help and training) has stimulated some criticism, and this has been reinforced by government concern about costs. Pressures for economy and rationalization of service would seem to be reinforced by personnel shortages.

Even in the Netherlands we heard some doubts expressed, for example, about the wisdom of extending the training program to two years and gathered that the Ministry of Culture, Recreation, and Social Work does not quite share the conviction of the Education Ministry that this is a good move. The new policy would bring students into the training program at the age of sixteen, immediately after graduation from a domestic science high school program. In view of the high rate of attrition (about 25 percent per year, since these young women will soon be starting their own families), extension of the program may raise costs unrealistically. On the other hand, the view was expressed that perhaps there would be fewer losses to competing occupations if the students

3. This is approximately what the fee in Sweden would be, if all the costs of service provision were included. However, no one there is expected to pay a full fee for this service.

were attracted at an earlier age. It was also suggested that the extra educational time might be better used through extension of the general education.

One question about the home help or the homemaker–home health aide service that strikes the observer rather forcibly concerns its continuing viability in its present form, given its underlying theory, namely, replacement of the "good housewife." Large families are less common, family relations are changing, outside employment of mothers is increasing, technological reorganization of household management through greater use of convenience foods and new cleaning and food-processing methods may be combining to make the all-purpose "good housewife" obsolete. In the face of such tendencies, one should expect mounting pressures to rationalize the service in order to cut costs and economize the use of scarce labor. After all, there are relatively fewer middle-class families with personal cleaning and maid service than there were a decade ago, and the coverage is declining rapidly. The change is most marked in the United States, but is under way in all industrialized countries where domestic work is often defined as low-status or dirty work. In a normal home, someone must still take the role of "woman of the house," or there must be husband-wife sharing; but home care is less often a chosen form of employment. (The Netherlands has not yet felt this problem. Compared with most of industrialized Europe, relatively few of its women work, and home help employment is regarded as a good work opportunity.) In any case, the work pays relatively poorly and may suffer in fringe benefits as well. In the face of this it seems rather strange to attempt expansion of something like domestic service for the old or for the family in crisis.

Recognizing that home helps supply a universally needed service, but that the service should be rationalized and that there eventually may be a problem in recruiting people to the work in its more traditional forms, the Dutch have been experimenting with alternative arrangements. One is to send children as "guests" to another family if illness or emergency takes a parent away for a brief period. (This system corresponds to American neighborhood emergency standby foster home arrangements or small neighborhood shelters. Provision is limited and accountability difficult.) Another alternative is to use group all-day-care arrangements for the children while one parent is away, thus permitting the employed parent to continue to work. A third alternative is to arrange for a home help worker to cover several homes in an area with minimal service, performing essential chores while the children are cared for elsewhere, but not moving in.

These approaches deal with situations involving families with children. In situations involving the aged and the handicapped, where the service is part time, for a few days a week, there have been other experimental approaches. For example, a team arrives with truck and cleaning equipment, takes care of the apartment, and moves on, much as do commercial cleaning services which work on an hourly basis in the United States and whose higher fees and task-oriented, rather than personal-service–oriented, approach to the job seems to decrease the stigma, if any, of the work. Such service, of course, does not take care of the "friendly visiting," shopping, and case-finding functions of the home helps. Presumably, these would be covered by other aspects of the community service system, including volunteer visitors. Or, as in Sweden, the home help would continue to provide this part of the service, but some of the more onerous aspects such as heavy cleaning would be implemented by such specialized teams. Similarly, in the United States, Meals-on-Wheels might provide a supplement to or partial substitute for homemaker–home health aide service.

Our observations on the service in Sweden and the Netherlands, the international dialogue in this field, and national experimentation all seem to indicate that what we are really dealing with are three different service situations, even though they face similar tasks in meeting personal and environmental needs. One provides services for the aged, often needed only once or twice a week, for several hours at a time, but on a long-term basis. The second provides coverage for a mother (or father), often on an intensive but short-term basis, to keep the family together and avoid placement of the children. The third represents one of a "package" of home health services to hasten the return home from a hospital or institution, or to prevent such placement in the first place. In the United States these three services are most often provided through multiservice agencies, such as social service agencies, welfare departments, or family agencies, or through health agencies, community nursing agencies, or hospital outpatient clinics. Increasingly, however, the service is provided through free-standing homemaker–home health aide service agencies. Approximately 26 percent of the more than 1,700 agencies in the United States and Canada responding to a 1973 survey by the National Council for Homemaker–Home Health Aide Services were such homemaker—home health aide agencies, and slightly over one-half of these were under public auspices.

Our best child welfare programs have demonstrated ingenuity in offering family coverage with homemakers, standby foster homes, day homes, and the like. But all of it is on a small scale. Medicaid-Medicare took a step forward in helping some people meet the cost of service but did not cope with service availability and delivery. Indeed, Medicare set up a self-defeating rule under which the service is reimbursable only as a postinstitutional measure.

In short, provision in this country has not yet absorbed the realities— that family emergencies are normal, occurring at predictable rates in all social strata, that senior citizens can be sustained in the community with specified services, and that a homemaker–home health aide program is a basic social utility which can be developed and administered on a scale and in a fashion to suit the American scene. Perhaps the time for major movement has arrived.

6

Family Vacations

in France

ALMOST thirty miles from Paris, on the edge of a national forest, we drove along a winding and beautifully landscaped road, through a park and wooded areas, to Dourdan, a specially designed, constructed, and government-aided family vacation resort. Dourdan contains a wide range of facilities for sports and recreational activities— tennis courts, trails for walking, hiking, and climbing, space for loafing, tranquil wooded glens for privacy—almost anything an individual might want in the course of his vacation.

Unlike many other social tourism facilities, Dourdan is not a converted private estate or home, but was built expressly to meet the needs and objectives of the French social tourism program. A large central pavilion houses the public facilities and administrative offices. The upper floors contain both single and double rooms; on the ground floor is a spacious lobby like those found in many middle-class resorts in the United States. Easy chairs and coffee tables are arranged in small groups, conducive to conversation and socializing. Nearby is a large bar (no hard liquor, just beer, wine, and soft drinks) and a service desk for sale of tickets, souvenirs, postcards, and the like. Off the lobby are a large auditorium and theater, dining rooms for adults and children, a self-service dining room for under-fives attended by an adult (older siblings, parents, and grandparents help out here), a language-teaching room with earphones and tape equipment (English instruction was being introduced), a nursery equipped with cribs for infant naps, arts and crafts workshops. The decor throughout is tasteful; everything is polished and in excellent repair.

In addition to the pavilion accommodations, there are individual and private family living quarters of one or more rooms (this is defined as "self-care"). They are landscaped, and blend into the extensive grounds the way lodges and cabins do in some American resorts.

Bulletin boards and posters announce program activities for the day and coming events. Some of these activities are included in the basic rate; in other cases separate fees must be paid. There are theater groups and entertainments, nature walks, concerts, dances, cultural trips to Paris. The latter is one of the attractions of this particular location for guests from the provinces.

We lunched with a family of four, who had arrived at the same time we did. Lunch was served at large tables. The chilled melon, steak, salad, cheese, and fresh fruit met their approval and ours. The wine we ordered had to be paid for separately; it is not included in the standard all-inclusive rate. The family told us that this is their second "season." Their children made friends here last summer with another family, expected to arrive shortly.

A few days later, we were in a small town only about a dozen miles from a metropolitan area. We drove up to an old mansion, set well back from a residential street. On arrival we were greeted in friendly fashion by a middle-aged man with a couple of children in tow, who introduced himself as a Dominican worker-priest, spending his vacation away from the factory. The house had been acquired through a legacy from the parents of the present directress of the "boardinghouse." She is a woman of perhaps sixty, president of a small family association under whose auspices the house is operated. She is a friendly person, and despite a touch of *grande dame* in manner, she seemed to maintain a warm relationship with the guests. The lower floors of the house contain a kitchen, large living and dining rooms, and a television, and, with original furnishings undisturbed, have the look of a solid bourgeois mansion.

The guests (with the exception of the priest) are family groups with children, with one or both parents present. With some exceptions, depending on size, families are lodged in one room, very plainly furnished. We judged the families, perhaps fifteen in all, to be of low income. Two were North Africans; one was a working-class mother of nine who, as her older children left school, fostered handicapped children, and who still seemed to be busy with several children. In general, in dress and demeanor, these are working people of modest means. A monitor, a youth of perhaps eighteen, takes charge of the children at mealtimes, and supervises play periods, takes them swimming to the town pool, and the like. Behind the house there is an impressive amount of land attached to the property, with gardens, trees, ample space for children and adults to rest or play games. Indoor playrooms, very roughly appointed, are located in supplementary buildings, perhaps old stables and tool rooms.

Families care for their own rooms and take turns at setting tables and bringing in platters of food. Meals are taken *en famille* at a long table, the directress at the head. Guests also help with dishwashing on Sundays. Lunch was excellent—chilled melon, braised fresh beef tongue, potato puree, cheese, and fresh peaches and pears. Roast beef had originally been scheduled, but was switched lest we think that a special menu had been arranged. After lunch the group retired to a circle of chairs arranged under a tree in the garden, and the cook, a hearty Breton lady, joined us for coffee. Babies and toddlers were dandled. The atmosphere was relaxed and pleasant; the keynote seemed to be rest and quiet rather than activity.

It is surprising how similar the two lunches were, here and at Dourdan. This and the child care arrangements are the common observable elements. In all these facilities we were impressed by the array of help provided for mothers so that their vacations are genuine: freedom from details of child care, restaurant meal service (children separate from adults), washing machines. Breakfast is served in the dining room, but the "makings" may be furnished for breakfast in one's apartment, which allows the kind of flexibility that makes a true vacation. Some facilities (*les gites*) which provide housekeeping units with kitchenettes may have a "telerestaurant" service, which offers a *plat du jour* for home consumption.

Our first question was: Why such a fuss about nice, middle-class vacation resorts, which are already in existence in the United States and elsewhere? Why would we have been urged to highlight French family vacations as a significant social service? Two aspects seem particularly interesting. First, although the guests resemble those at similar resorts in the United States, a good many are enjoying subsidized payments, even subsidized fares to the resort area. Second, there is an ideology, a goal, an intent, perhaps a mystique, about the whole vacation program; each facility has programed activities which the French call *animation*.

This concept has no English equivalent, but the ambiance of *animation* is conveyed by the fact that, in general, many social service and social welfare programs in France are guided by a sense of communal solidarity—the old mutual aid of family and the cooperative effort of local neighborhood translated into national endeavor. Americans establish family services for charitable and humanistic reasons and out of a sense of social justice. The French add to this a highly valued "solidarity."

That solidarity includes the notion that family members, occupied during the year with school, work, or household tasks, should have the opportunity (have a *right* to the opportunity) to enjoy one another's company, to find diversion and stimulation through social programs. The goals are encompassed by such imprecise concepts (whether French or English) as the broadening of tastes; the experiencing of unfamiliar cultural, athletic, or collective activities; self-realization in new realms. *Animation* is the encouragement of such development and experience by providing opportunity and, perhaps, by an enabling, supportive type of staffing.

All these places share a dedication to this vaguely realized aim, a concept difficult for Americans. At times, however, one senses a striving for collectivity or community, while at other times something more concrete seems involved. For example, reference to *equipes d'animation* seems to translate as "program staff." *Animation sportive* at Dourdan refers to tennis, football, judo, and fencing for children; riding, archery, and swimming for everyone. And the *animation générale* covers such activities as workshops for arts and crafts, games, dances, discussion, and excursions to Rambouillet, Versailles, Chartres, Paris. And yet, perhaps, "something more" seems to struggle for expression. The director of Dourdan said that it is difficult to sustain the spirit of the policy ideal at a cultural and self-development level that differentiates it from commercial offerings. As a matter of fact the comment was made that where *animation* is really needed is in helping people get to know the vacation possibilities open to them.

But why include a report on family vacations in a listing of programs that might have something to say to the United States? Even the French term "social tourism," applied to these programs, sounds strange to the American ear. Is the objective to "socialize" vacations in the sense that costs are shared between society and the individual, and resource disparities equalized? Or is the emphasis on program goals a social objective similar to that addressed by the "social director" of some large American resort hotels? The synonym "family vacations" is frequently employed. Somewhat clearer, it certainly strikes a more familiar note.

Contrary to our expectations, French "social tourism" or "family vacations" is not yet meeting the goals of its French sponsors. Indeed, some of the goals may not be as sharply defined as we had expected. Yet, if our explorations raised many questions about the French program, they also drew attention to an arena of social policy not much discussed in the United States. Perhaps it is not the most important of all subjects in a world in which there is hunger, inflation, unemployment, and homelessness, but it is not one to be dismissed.

Robert Perlman of Brandeis University, in one of the few major serious discussions of the subject as a social policy topic for the United States, recently commented that at a time of a do-it-yourself approach to social problems and human needs it is probably perversely utopian to talk about a public policy on vacations. Nonetheless, leisure is clearly a future arena for debate and action. It is estimated that, before long, vacation time will constitute 16 percent of Americans' nonworking, nonsleeping time. Americans who earn or buy vacations do quite well. Some industrialized nations intervene to help those who cannot take vacations on their own. Thus, the question arises: Should those who now get no vacation under the rules of the game be aided in some way? Should there be "organized provisions to insure poor and otherwise disadvantaged Americans a respite from the tensions and tumult of contemporary living which affect us all, certainly not least the lowest status group in our society"?[1]

The French Have a Program for It

To the foreign tourist, Paris appears empty of Frenchmen in August. Small wonder: government reports show that 76 percent of all Parisians take vacations. The rate is far lower in rural areas (17 percent). While vacation take-up has grown steadily since World War II, the rate of increase, perhaps even the absolute percentage, is declining as the percentages of immobile aged and young homemakers who are saving for other purposes grows.

In 1972, over 46 percent of all French people took vacations. Several other European countries show even higher percentages. U.S. reports tell us that 20 to 40 percent of all American families do not take vacations at all in a year. In fact, over a quarter of all Americans have never taken a vacation. Of those who do vacation in a given year, two-thirds enjoy two weeks or less. These findings are similar to those in reports from six European countries. About a quarter of all families (U.S. and European surveys) now vacation more than once each year. Among the vacationers, 25 percent of the British, almost 36 percent of the French, and perhaps a similar proportion of Americans who go away

1. Robert Perlman, "Vacations—for Whom?" *Social Policy*, July-Aug. 1973. This source lists major studies of U.S. vacation benefits and programs and is the major single concise reference we could locate. Perlman documents our U.S. statistical citations.

from home spend their time with friends or relatives. All American research documents the fact that the elderly, the uneducated, and those with low incomes are least likely to vacation or, if they do, they go for away-from-home vacations far less often than other Americans. Similarly, nonwhites leave home when they vacation less often than do whites.

The French stress vacations for all as a goal. In the words of one informant: "Everybody agrees—and the government confirms it periodically—that the need for vacations is as fundamental as sanitation or housing. This means the right to vacations for all." The average French vacation duration, 26.5 days, leads the industrialized world. There is significant help with vacation opportunity for low-income workers and others. The evolution of the commitment and practice therefore is of interest.

French social tourism began officially in 1936, when the Léon Blum government enacted legislation guaranteeing workers two weeks of paid vacation. According to French sources this was extraordinarily significant to the working class, since it was defined as opening the door "to rest and escape into the country, into life." The more prosperous saw this as the time when beaches were first invaded by workers in caps and picnic gear. What the law did, of course, was to guarantee an annual rest period, not an away-from-home vacation. The social tourism programs deal with ways of subsidizing (1) facilities, (2) individuals, or (3) travel, so as to permit the away-from-home vacation, as well as (4) ways of giving that vacation the content described as *animation*. An American wonders about all these elements as he attempts to interpret U.S. data.

The real push for public provision began in France after World War II. Our French informant writes:

The country longed to live again. Organizations for families, religion, workers, youth, and under-privileged, as well as boards of directors of large enterprises, arranged with whatever they had to send children off to vacation camps (already numerous before the war). They also tried to find lodgings for parents who wanted to leave with their children. Middle-class villas rented at low prices or given up by their owners, old farms fixed up more or less to receive families, or large tents . . . with basic sanitary equipment, received families at the ocean or lakes, in the country, and in the mountains. The end of a difficult period, the joy of being on vacation, and the town spirit made one forget the lack of comfort. . . . But the period of hardiness did not last long.

More had to be done in response to increasing enthusiasm for vacations, more vacation rights in labor union contracts, and the recognition that available income would not offer some families access to facilities produced in the marketplace. A pattern of *material assistance* (subsidized construction and operation) and of *individual assistance* (financial aid to the poorest) has permitted development of major new initiatives.

Currently, French governmental efforts focus on increasing four types of facilities: houses for family vacations, vacation villages, independent vacation cottages, and family campgrounds. The responsible national authorities are the Department of Public Health (for the "houses") and the Government Office for Tourism (for the rest). Regional public authorities enforce standards. Each type of facility, we believe, has an American counterpart.

Houses for family vacations constitute the oldest of the programs. The establishments are nonprofit and allow parents to take vacations with their children. Reserved for low-income families, the houses are required to offer facilities comparable to hotels in the areas, but at lower charges.

Each house has eighty to two hundred beds. Families are assigned one or two rooms according to size. Bath and toilet facilities are usually available for each family, too, but are sometimes shared. Among the shared "public" facilities are kitchen and dining room, recreation rooms, a child-care service (with a paid attendant, unless parents rotate in that responsibility), informal public rooms, often a playground. Families take care of their own rooms. In some places they assist in kitchen tasks. The daily life is informal and intimate.

Vacation villages appeared at the end of the 1950s. Living quarters are scattered among anywhere from two to ten buildings. A central building has the shared and public facilities: kitchen, adult and child restaurants, child-care service, laundry, entertainment room, playrooms, meeting rooms, and library. Playgrounds and swimming (and boating), riding, or climbing facilities are also shared. The accommodations include a living-bedroom for parents, one or two children's rooms, toilet and bath facilities. Capacities range from three hundred to one thousand.

Although here, too, families maintain their own apartments, the more comfortable conveniences, increased services, and more elaborate recreation resources lead to higher costs than at the family vacation homes.

Unlike hotels (that is, marketplace hotels) both family houses and villages offer child-care services and expect visitors to participate in the housekeeping. Moreover, their staff consider it their task to create a "welcome" atmosphere and interaction among guests, much as the program staff do in many American resorts.

Independent vacation cottages represent a new pattern that removes the central eating arrangements from the vacation villages and transfers them to the individual cottages. The family cottage is equipped with refrigeration, stove, and dishes. There is a take-out service for hot dinners, if desired, but most families live on their own, so costs are lower.

Family campgrounds resemble the facilities available in many national parks, state parks, and private trailer camps in the United States. Families are given access to approved campgrounds on which they may pitch their tents or park their trailers, or may rent equipment on the spot. Other facilities and arrangements are similar to those for independent cottages, but costs are still lower. Camping is the "preferred" vacation of the lowest-income families—often all they can afford.

What makes the French vacation program interesting to us, then, is not the facilities per se. Each type is known in the United States; even *animation* in many places at least seems much like the social and recreational programing supplied by many American resorts. The unique characteristic of the French program is its determination to expand resources, keep prices down, and offer access to particular groups beyond what the workings of the normal free marketplace for recreation and vacations probably would accomplish.

The facilities are not, however, government-run. Operating groups may be churches, lay associations, employee groups, consumer cooperatives, community groups, regional family allowance offices. Material assistance is of four kinds: public funding, credit from communities, subscription funds, and self-financing.

Public funds are available from a number of sources. Two government ministries are authorized to provide subsidies for the construction of facilities. The Department of Public Health is concerned with family vacation homes, and the Government Office for Tourism helps with funding for vacation villages, family cottages, and campgrounds. The former department may offer subsidies for up to 40 percent of the building and equipment costs, the latter up to 30 percent—in theory. Appropriations actually available keep the subsidies at 15 and 10 percent, respectively.

Other public subsidies may come from the Department of Agriculture, which hopes to boost the economies of underdeveloped rural areas by encouraging tourism; the National Office for Family Allowances, to create resources for its beneficiary constituencies; and the Government

Tourist Office program, to add to resources in underequipped areas. The sum total of subsidies is limited to 60 percent of building and equipment costs. In addition, there are public loans, generally at low interest rates.

Credit from communities, though less substantial, is also available. Town authorities may offer modest assistance to attract facilities, or may offer a free site in return for ownership of the facility after sixty years.

Subscription funds collected by public, semiprivate, and private organizations often meet up to one-third of the cost of a facility in return for special utilization rights for members, but not special rates. These participating groups may be employee organizations, retirement funds, or voluntary insurance groups. If the participation is sizable, it assures not only priorities but also representation on the facility's management board.

Self-financing may, of course, also be practiced. The nonprofit sponsor may raise its own funds, but seldom meets more than 10 percent of its costs in this fashion.

In 1970, all these sources of grants, subsidies, and loans totaled the equivalent of $50 million at current exchange rates. Half of it came from employee organizations.

In the debate as to whether to assist the facility or the individual, the French have decided to do both. Thus, at least five devices for individual assistance are available.

One is *paid vacation tickets*. Once a year, workers or retired workers and their families may benefit from a 30 percent fare reduction for a train trip of at least 120 miles, round trip.

Employee vacation bonuses may also be offered. Many employers distribute yearly vacation bonuses which are either fixed sums or a percentage of salary. The value of the bonus varies tremendously from company to company, and is, in any case, unrelated to family need.

Vacation allowances, on the other hand, are related to need. In some companies, employee organizations give vacation allowances to the lowest-paid workers.

Vacation certificates, too, are needs-tested, since these vouchers are offered either by family allowance regional offices or by some of the independent social security offices (National Railroad Company) or banks. For example, the family allowance offices gives certificates to low-income families with at least two children. But there are 111 different family offices each with its own policies, and the certificate grants are generally limited.

Finally, *adjusted rates* which reflect income as well as number and ages of children are often offered by the social tourism facilities themselves.

It is readily noted that a system as diverse and complex as this breeds considerable inequity. One's family allowance office, region, job, union, choice of facility, income, family composition, and enterprise all determine what is available. Some low-income families benefit from several allowances and, in effect, have free vacations. Others suffer "notch" effects: just over the eligibility level, they get nothing, even though they cannot afford commercial vacations. Similarly, some people by virtue of location in a particular enterprise or within a specific distance from resorts do quite well, while others get only token help.

Equity among Social Classes?

The French commitments interest us as a way of opening vacation opportunities to those who do not now enjoy them. Yet the pattern has its own built-in problems in this regard.

We noted the difference between Dourdan and the small-town vacation house. The former is a modern resort, effectively competing in its amenities with the commercial sector (and, its sponsors believe, adding the *animation* ingredient). The latter is a simpler country "boardinghouse" of a type which is disappearing with the growth of affluence.

Without careful research it would be unwise to venture an opinion about the degree of social integration that is encouraged or achieved in either. The boardinghouse, clearly, is not Dourdan: in the one, cotton housedresses and in the other "leisure clothes"; in the one, the welcome of the worker-priest, apparently happy to have a couple of children to look out for, and in the other, as it happened, also a welcome from a guest on arrival—a carefully dressed woman of sixty-five or seventy who volunteered that she had been vacationing at Dourdan for four years, was now at point of retiring, and was absolutely delighted with the facility. There are significant differences of decor, style, tone, equipment, and manner, and they bespeak class differences. There may, of course, be crossclass integration within Dourdan, masked by accommodation and adaptation to a common style, but the guests look homogeneous. Rates are scaled to income, but the lowest rate still seems burdensome for a low-income family, despite subsidies and benefits that may accrue under different collective wage contracts and other sources of family benefits.

Social tourism can hardly claim to offer something to all low-income families.[2] In fact, barely half of all families who use these facilities have low incomes. Because of costs, some places must scale their rates so that only middle-income people are able to meet them. Some places have only low-income people in July and August but are taken over completely by the more prosperous during the Christmas and Easter holidays. This is especially true of mountain installations with skiing facilities. What social tourism does for these more prosperous groups is to permit enjoyment of a second semisubsidized winter vacation after a summer vacation in the commercial market.

The major nonprofit organization in the field, V.V.F., or Villages, Vacances, Familles (Villages, Vacations, Families), surveyed its own experience for the 1966–71 period and noted that—as compared with their percentages in the population at large—blue-collar workers are underrepresented by about one-third in V.V.F. villages and cottages, whereas white-collar and middle-management personnel are heavily overrepresented and agricultural personnel much underrepresented.

To the observer, the French program of social tourism appears to be faced with several problems and choices. It wants to improve facilities and amenities to meet growing affluence in the society at large, yet to do so raises costs and affects the class mix. Management analysts suggest year-round plant operation to amortize large investments more quickly, but these social programs are not intended to compete with the commercial tourist business, which fears that programs outside July and August might steal clients. To cover overhead, an "off season" catering to the retired aged is promoted, but experts in social gerontology have asked whether the programs represent the best use of resources or are even helpful. Finally, the *animation* and self-realization targets involve costs which managers concerned with budgets find it harder to justify. To an American the *animation* would seem to create an institutional character that might affect facility attractiveness, but we do not know how it appears to the French.

The director of Dourdan, an energetic young administrator, spoke frankly of the effect of economic constraints on policy. The need to operate within budgetary limitations affects intake policy. That policy is supposed to favor economically weak families and those with several

2. Given the rate of vacationing and the concentration of such vacationers in fixed periods during July and August each year, the following data about bed capacities are relevant: hotels, 1,500,000; family houses, 50,000; villages and cottages, 66,000; private houses, 740,000; rental of private houses, 1,800,000; camping grounds, 1,150,000. All social tourism programs, then, have a capacity of 5,306,000 beds for a population of some 51 million.

children, but the socioeconomic composition of the applicants cannot be disregarded lest the budget be imperiled. The economic burden of maintaining a competent year-round staff in the large installations necessitates year-round use of the facilities (outside school holiday periods) for conferences, seminars, meetings, and weekends for singles and couples aged eighteen to thirty-five and for old people, individually or in groups organized by social service, company, or trade union committees. Family weekends are also available and a brochure speaks glowingly of the convenience of leasing a second home for regular weekend use during the period from October to June, with possessions left in place and arrangements for advance heating available if desired.

In the meantime, France's Sixth Plan, now well along, aims at an additional 330,000 places in campgrounds and 35,000 beds in villages and cottages. Funds invested in social tourism in only one organization, CNAF, grew from about $5.4 million in 1970 to $12 million in 1973. National expenditure data are not available. A designated committee is seeking to simplify procedures to finance construction of facilities. Several influential political bodies are urging a larger measure of public subsidy and the setting aside of more of the most desirable sites for social tourism installations before they are taken over completely for commercial usage. Efforts are being made to stagger vacations as well, permitting a changeover from a pattern in which most vacation centers are used only eighty-five days a year and are thus very expensive to run. However, cultural patterns already deeply established and the resultant tendency of many businesses, especially in France and in Scandinavia, to close down completely in vacation periods will limit what can be accomplished in this regard. Only increased year-round usage for other purposes will help, and this is feasible in a world in which conference holding, continuing education, health entitlements, and programs for the elderly are increasing.

Presumably these and related matters are within the scope of the five coordinating groups in France, national federations in which the various associations of facilities or sponsors share problems, develop standards, and promote resources. These groups, in turn, are represented in a national commission in this field and also cooperate with the efforts of an international bureau. Increasingly, Europeans cross national borders at vacation time. Northern Europeans, for example, rely heavily upon the Mediterranean area for sunshine.

Convinced that vacations are a public good, even a necessity, there are those who would focus their efforts on increasing the vacation resources available to individuals. More groups are encouraged to give vacation assistance to low-income families. More companies are urged to give the vacation bonus. And note is taken of the practice of double pay at vacation time in some firms in Belgium. There is also experiment with "vacation stamps" redeemed by employer associations, so that a man is not penalized for changing jobs. The family allowance offices in the regions are helping more people learn about facilities and the ways in which they, as individuals, may be aided. Note is taken, too, of another Belgian system: an extra family allowance grant in May, for vacations. A special vacation allowance, like the means-tested housing allowance, also is debated, but opponents ask who will pay for it. Public authorities are said to be considering and experimenting with a Swiss-type "vacation check" (the employer, in effect, supplements the worker's set-aside vacation money, but only modestly).

The outside observer is struck by the dedication to vacation time, the increased tendency to travel and to use facilities organized for recreation—as opposed to relatives' households. In accord with policy, there is less demand for places to send children and more call for places for family units. Certainly the facts are there, but it is not clear from afar or from available analyses how much of this tendency stems from public demand for opportunities not available commercially and how much is due to activity by the government and nonprofit enterprise and could be supplied by the commercial market. Nor is it completely clear whether changing tastes, increasing use of automobiles for family touring, other changes in life styles, or changing government policies are directly or indirectly influencing family behavior.

It is certainly not clear—and this is most crucial—whether *animation* makes a qualitative difference, a contribution to French family policy, or is merely an ideology and rationale for a program of much-needed recreation and vacations which are not qualitatively different from what Americans know. And, indeed, if education, development, self-realization are promoted and effective, would a culture such as ours regard this as an appropriate social service target or as a debatable paternalism?

Any American Connection?

In the mid-nineteenth century, United States "child-saving" agencies began to place homeless or otherwise vulnerable children with farm families to remove them from the hazards of city life. Cities had long been considered evil. Later, camps for poor children, whether healthy or ill, were developed, with similar premises. Social service vacations, then, were designed to offer health, renewal, an environment for re-cuperation. To this the "character-building" groups, the scouts, boys' clubs, religious societies, and so on, added a more elaborate rationale about experience which created desirable character traits.

Children's camps, in any case, became a major enterprise of voluntary philanthropy in the United States. Some settlement houses did a modest amount of family vacation development, offering cottages or rooms in a large house, usually for two weeks, to very deprived families and on a very limited scale. Gradually, too, small but often innovative and creative camp and summer resort programs developed for the physically handicapped, including the blind, and for a modest number of the aged. The 1960s saw further development of youth and family programs, some of them with ethnic-racial content or developmental and skill goals, some of them quite innovative, but with limited duration and capacity.

Since the Great Depression, and particularly since World War II, as America has taken to the road and to the air, there has been enormous development of expensive vacation resorts on the mainland, in Hawaii, in the Caribbean, mostly for the middle class and well-to-do, but not solely. National park and state park facilities continue to grow and to be crowded. Youth travel in the middle and late teens has become a large industry and crosses class lines.

By now over 90 percent of organized American workers have vacation coverage in their contracts, almost three-fourths of the entitlements reaching four weeks after sufficient time on the job. In the steel, aluminum, and automobile industries there are even sabbatical and extended vacations reaching ten to thirteen weeks in duration. Children, middle-class or poor, do not do badly, with philanthropy imitating affluence at least in assuring access to some away-from-home facility, even if closer and less luxurious than the resort-camps of the richly endowed. Many in the professions and in business also may enjoy job-related and at least partially deductible resort vacations and overseas trips in connection with business travel, professional meetings, conventions, and professional education. But the unorganized, the low-paid, the hourly workers, the aged without social insurance, and the large families either have no entitlements or have too many burdens to enjoy their entitlements. It may be that public welfare programs finance vacations in some places, but data are hard to come by and totals will not be large.

Some Americans do not enjoy escape, recoupment opportunity, "fresh air," self-realization, relaxation in an attractive environment. Thus, there are some among the more affluent, the "work addicts," who are exceptions to the otherwise solid correlations between income, education, occupation, and vacations, just as there are those in all groups who do not want to vacation away from home. But it is clear that insufficient resources and limited opportunity do deprive significant numbers of people in the United States of vacations, particularly among the old, the poor, the unskilled, the minority group members.

In all of this we are similar to the Europeans. But, as noted in United Nations reports and the work of international organizations (and putting our French report in context), there are differences, both qualitative and quantitative, that we in this country might do well to consider: (1) a stress on the right to a good vacation, so that the duration is longer and efforts are made to help with costs; (2) the use of trips to the south (Majorca and the Canary Islands, for example) for health and recovery purposes, usually for older people, often as a social insurance or health plan benefit, as in Denmark and Sweden; (3) subsidized train fares in vacation periods for families of very low income, as in France and Italy; (4) special vacation bonuses or grants or supplements through the job or the family allowance (social security) office, as in France; (5) a tendency to see even the job-related vacation bonus as a social benefit available as a worker right, not as a seniority payment, so that the new worker enjoys it as much as the old (indeed, in some places the worker carries his rights from job to job by means of vacation stamps); and (6) a policy which protects the commercial vacation industry but assumes that many people, not just "the poor," will not be able to enjoy their leisure unless there are also nonprofit subsidized facilities provided.

In the United States, as in many other places, millions of people get no vacations at all because, as Perlman has noted, the paid vacation "was designed for wage earners and it remains tied, conceptually and practically, to the worker's employment record." In a statement of general aspirations of many people for a better life, the U.N. Declaration of Human Rights announces that "everyone has the right to rest and leisure." The French have apparently taken that notion most seriously and tied the rationale to family policy, as have other Europeans.

None of this, per se, argues for a larger or smaller commercial or nonprofit vacation resource component in the United States. Ultimately it is necessary to decide whether resources are in short supply or are inaccessible to some people—or, perhaps, whether certain types of programs will not appear unless created as public merit goods. For that matter, we must decide whether we believe that social tourism enriches the lives of members of families and other people in such significant ways that it should have a high priority for the United States.

It is clear that national parks are crowded, perhaps overcrowded, as are state park camp sites. They are inaccessible for the most part, except to people who own cars or can hitch-hike. Perhaps they need more rapid expansion. It is urgent to discover, too, whether resources are in short supply generally for people who cannot meet the costs of vacations produced in the marketplace. And we must learn whether people who can pay modest sums can fund what they want—or need—and what the public wants them to have. As these and related matters are pursued, several questions arise:

Should more facilities be subsidized by government, to put them within the price range of poorer people? Do middle-income people also require subsidized facilities? Are there some more resources which can be protected for the public only through public policy?

Should social security or supplementary security income or public assistance subsidize individual vacations in the future, the way private philanthropy long has, but cannot do on a large scale for families? Would the beneficiaries be solely the poor—or others too, especially among the aged?

Should health insurance systems be more generous in covering health-related vacation trips, particularly for senior citizens?

Should family-oriented vacation resources be given increasing weight as a matter of public policy? What weight should be given to the traditional camps for children? to the expanding programs for adolescents? What is the balance? The United States has no family policy in the French sense; from where would our criteria derive?

Should the mandatory vacation legislation of several European countries be copied in the United States? Should entitlement be separated from seniority, as it often is in Europe, on the assumption that it is a social benefit needed by all? If so, could it be vested in the worker?

Although we have no equivalent of family allowance funds, as do the French or the Belgians, ought we to supplement vacation funds for poor families with children as do these countries through some income maintenance device? or perhaps for all families with several children? or for youth as a category?

And do we in the United States want to tie ideology to family vacations (our equivalent of French *animation*) as we once did to children's camps? If not, how might we sponsor a system while protecting current diversity and options?

In short, are these important questions for us? Are they issues? Are they interesting? Should we in the United States begin to discuss a public policy for vacations?

7

Housing for the Elderly

in Sweden

SUN CITY, Arizona, is building ten new homes a day. For its population of 30,000, it is offering six shopping centers, nine golf courses, five extravagant recreation centers, an indoor pool and shuffleboard courts, a synthetic-surfaced lawn bowling green, an amphitheater, a stadium, two lakes, and a two-hundred–bed hospital.[1] Yet this is a strange, new type of community, an age-segregated suburb for the elderly. Despite predictions that old people would not be interested and, in fact, would suffer if such plans were carried out, dozens of new "retirement" towns and developments have sprung up on the outskirts of urban areas throughout the country, but especially where the climate is usually sunny, dry, and warm. Newspaper reports, television promotions, word of mouth, bring new prospects by the thousands.

Or there is Rossmoor–Walnut Creek in Berkeley, California, a secure, guarded condominium, with apartments for seven thousand, located on a former ranch site.[2] A search for security, good climate, freedom from burdens of home care, and a new pattern of life attracts retirees. But here, as in Sun City, the resources are for the affluent. So are they in Rossmoor, New Jersey, which features detached homes, and at the Sequoian, a three hundred–apartment, high-rise "life-time care" facility in San Francisco, where the initial payment is as much as one would pay for a good house and there is an additional monthly fee.

The half-million people in the United States in such adult communities, retirement villages, and life-time care facilities are middle-income, according to Sheila K. Johnson; this means they have access to

1. See *New York Times*, March 24, 1974.
2. See Sheila K. Johnson in *New York Times Magazine*, November 11, 1973.

$30,000–$65,000 for investment and $10,000 in annual income. Those who prefer city-based "life-time care facilities," like the Sequoian, pay $55,000 or more for a small apartment, three restaurant meals a day, paid-up medical care—and assurance that they will have help and care for the rest of their natural lives (although they must be sure to draw whatever medical and income maintenance benefits their incomes and situations allow). Another 1.5 million retirees, with smaller incomes, live in trailer parks.

All this is the tip of a larger iceberg—a visible part of a community-care "movement" for the aged. The movement is as much a reaction to excessive hospitalization of the aged and their removal to large congregate care facilities under one guise or another, as it is to the allegedly excessive use of, and the horrors reported about, large numbers of American nursing homes. More basically it reflects increased longevity, earlier retirement, and increased physical well-being for longer periods of time after retirement. In the social agency (non-market) sector, public and voluntary, the "movement" includes apartments for old people in public housing, buildings for retirees, new types of old age homes, senior citizen centers, home health visitors, congregate eating, and the like. America is searching, experimenting, debating—and wanting to learn.

Developments in Sweden, of course, have their counterparts among the many interesting American developments. But Sweden is dedicated to a novel policy: "Everyone should feel secure." People have a right to a minimum income, essential health care, good housing, easy access to services. These principles, backed up by government policy and the taxes to pay for it, have led to a considerable development of community living arrangements for everyone. And it is this emphasis on *everyone* rather than the prosperous middle class alone which is interesting. We have noted earlier, of course, that Sweden is a very small and homogeneous country and therefore not a precise model for the United States, but a review of what Sweden is doing helps define the issues for the rest of us.

From the first we observed that there is no "retirement village" movement in Sweden. Indeed, after a post–World War II flurry, the development of separate communities for the aged has declined or disappeared in northern Europe. Sweden's slogan is "normalization": basic needs should be met in forms which come as near as possible to the forms under which other members of society live; if possible, the facilities should be located within the "ordinary society."

Huddinge

We begin in Huddinge, an independent municipality of 90,000 people south of Stockholm. Huddinge is a young community. Only 5 percent of its residents are retirees, while the figure is 10–15 percent elsewhere in the country.

We talked to Mrs. L., an eighty-year-old woman living in a "service flat" in an area called Vårbygård (Spring Village Farm). A service flat is an ordinary apartment, rented from the local social welfare authorities, who maintain fifty-one such flats in a block of four multiple-dwelling buildings. The flats for the aged, constituting one-third of the total, are concentrated in groups but are in building units occupied by young families. The term service house is employed to indicate that the building has special shared facilities for residents, so that the old person (or the young couples, or handicapped tenants) are not limited to what the apartment holds. Our hostess commented that she was delighted with the flat: "I've worked hard all my life. Now I can rest. But I have a choice. If I want to cook myself, I can do it in my kitchenette. If I am lazy and want company, I go to join my neighbors in this corridor and eat in the dining room. If I want to be alone, I close my door. If I need some help or care, I can phone or press the signal button to the hostess of the service center. I feel so secure here."

Many of the men and women we interviewed expressed this sense of security. But they were not referring to security against theft or assault as they would be in the United States. They meant confidence about access to help, resources, human considerateness.

In Huddinge, "senior citizens" may eat noon meals in the schools after the children are served, and at a low fee. One hundred do daily. Mrs. L.'s service house is opposite a gaily colored new school building with an extremely attractive, comfortable cafeteria. Only ten senior citizens eat here daily, but the cafeteria workers enjoy chatting with them and regard it as a social occasion.

The Huddinge service flats for the aged are integrated into tastefully designed, colorful, multiple dwellings, with a shopping center and other amenities nearby. Residents can walk to the lake and boat harbor or observe the glass-walled swimming pool in the school. Mrs. L. has easy access to a modest community center. Her alarm system is connected to their switchboard.

The center is in a well-designed, yet modest, building. To the right of the entrance foyer there is a cloakroom and there is a cafeteria which the people in the service flats and staff use at subsidized prices. Doors here and in the apartments are easily negotiated by wheel chairs. There are a few small but well-used hobby shops—textiles, wood—and rooms for beauty parlor, foot care, and special baths. These are present in most Swedish centers. The scale is comfortable and the relationships between "users" and staff obviously good. Besides service flat residents, the center is used by other aged citizens from the vicinity. Neither the flats nor the center has a high staffing requirement, partly because the locality also has 230 part-time home helps.

While policy varies by community, this municipality—as others— offers retirees a housing allowance on a "means-test" basis. In effect, a single person who has only the basic pension and lives in a one-room service flat has his entire rent paid. This is also true of a retired couple in a two-room flat.

Sundbyberg

The service flat is not the only possible housing arrangement. Old and new models are visible in Sundbyberg, only eleven minutes from downtown Stockholm by train or a little longer by bus. This working-class suburb has a population of 29,000, of whom 10 percent are over sixty-seven. It has a progressive social service tradition. Three "old people's" houses are maintained: Mariagården, for 26 residents; Lötsjogården for 90; and Östergården for 144. Mariagården places its aged citizens on the second floor of a renovated home. The first floor is devoted to a day-care facility for thirty children and also to an alcoholics rehabilitation program. Dining room facilities are shared (and also used by neighborhood aged and handicapped residents), but the groups eat at different times.

A visit to Östergården (Eastern Farm) was instructive. Built in 1951, the low, two-story, red brick building is in a typical Sundbyberg neighborhood. Windows look out toward industry, homes, schools, street traffic, but the immediate environs are quiet. The three wings frame a beautifully landscaped internal garden, with a fountain and sitting space.

Although Östergården is an old age home or "nursing home," offering rooms and services rather than flats, it is popular. When Hallonbergen's new-style pensioners' center was built, tenants of Östergården were offered the opportunity to move to the more modern and comfortable environment. After visits, only two chose the new facility; the rest preferred the small-homelike environment of Östergården. Indeed, local residents of regular buildings and service flats also use many of the home's services.

Government policy favors service flats in "normal" housing or hotel-like arrangements (a building of flats for old people) but not these homes. It has abolished the state loans and subsidies for building old people's homes. Yet there are champions of small, warm, active homes like this one. Many old people, who live in flats far from relatives and friends and have home help a couple of hours per day or week, are very isolated for the rest of the time. The proponents of the home ask: Why not bring them together before they are too old for new contacts?

A visitor understands the enthusiasm. The lobby is like that of a private home; the atmosphere in the public rooms conveys the style and comfort of an earlier day and is warmer than many of Sweden's new, functionally modern facilities. There is a kiosk for beer, candy, and sundries near the entrance as well as an interesting and frequently changed museum exhibit in a case. The staff is enthusiastic, responsible, concerned. The sitting room and dining facility, where a resident may entertain guests or enjoy holiday meals on lovely old china, are traditionally furnished and most attractive.

This home is a very active place. The residents we visited appear to enjoy the program. The shop and workrooms display unusually fine handicrafts. Here and elsewhere in Sundbyberg participants arrange sales of what they make and now have access to about $3,600 annually, which has permitted them to buy a bus. There are now "trips" as often as three times a week, with the porter of Östergården serving as driver. Some of the residents, among others a ninety-year-old lady who had never been abroad until she came here, now also participate in cheap charter trips to Greece, Spain, Italy, and elsewhere in Europe.

Not all residents, of course, are healthy enough for trips, and some need considerable care. There is a special sick section, where a resident may remain for two to three months without loss of rights to his or her usual room. After that time the question may arise as to whether transfer to a nursing home or hospital is necessary. From 5 to 7 percent of the retirees in Sundbyberg are estimated to require hospitalization.

About 30 percent of the current residents in Östergården need what is called "heavy medical care." The costs are shared by the patients, the county authorities, and state subsidies to local authorities.

Pensioners pay fees, according to income, covering 18–20 percent of costs, state subsidies cover 35–40 percent, and the remainder is met by local government.

Residents pay rent at a rate which leaves about forty-five dollars monthly for pocket money for those with only a basic pension. The pensioners' fees vary between four and eleven dollars per day; daily operating costs are twenty-four dollars per pensioner.

Östergården has a three-shift staff of seventy-five part-time and full-time workers, plus a doctor who comes for six hours a week. The director is trained as a nurse and has also worked in psychiatric care and in administration. He has three assistants (who now take special one-year courses on management of living facilities for old people),[3] two trained nurses (one full-time and one half-time), five assistant nurses, and about thirty care attendants (with eight to twenty-four weeks of professional training). Kitchen staff consists of one administrator, two cooks, four kitchen assistants, and serving staff. There is also an advisory council of residents.

To many observers, Swedish and foreign, Östergården is an old age home. To its inventive and effective director it is a halfway house offering semi-open care. In any case, the locality is not now building what it would define as "separated" old age homes. It is investing far more heavily in community care—eating arrangements, centers, home helps, transportation—and in a combination of service flats in "normal housing," whether spread about or in small blocks, and buildings made up only of service flats and common facilities for old people ("pensioners' hotels"). Often these several approaches are combined administratively and physically as they are in some American experimental programs.

One of the more dramatic, newer Sundbyberg efforts is seen at Hallonbergen, a development near Lake Lötsjön. Here the goal is to achieve "normalization" by placing both old people's homes and service flats for retirees right in the activity center of the entire housing development. This appears to be the current preference in Sweden.

Some 2,283 flats are being built in five groups in the Hallonbergen area. One block contains flats for students or other young people;

---

3. Matrons provide both facility maintenance and program leadership in service houses and pensioners' hotels. The ones currently moving into such roles have completed special one-year courses given in five or six different places. Many have prior nursing training. Given the variety of specialties in the institutional and group service field, there is currently some debate in Sweden about appropriate training and conceptualization of specialties.

another has specially designed flats exclusively for old people and invalids. There are similar flats scattered in the rest of the houses, among ordinary flats for families, serving retired people who do not need the special services of the old people's home or special physical arrangements. Currently, since the aged population has not yet reached its expected level, some of the places in the old age home are rented to Stockholm people, and some of the special "service flat" apartments, scattered in several housing blocks, are rented to young couples.

The area has some light industry and commercial activity, as well as residences. It was planned with enormous care as a model community. The environment is oriented to the needs of invalids and old people: all entrances and walkways are negotiable by wheel chair; outside doors respond to radio signals; and there are terrain lifts and many de-iced walkways. The entire area, beautifully landscaped, makes excellent use of color, texture, and materials. From the parking area, one notes immediately the close proximity of, and easy connections among, the three "clusters"—school, facilities for the aged, shopping and commercial activities.

In the "old age home" wing, we visited the apartment of a ninety-year-old woman, Mrs. T. There is a good-size foyer, which has cabinets on the right and a small table. To the left is a bathroom. Directly ahead is the main living room–bedroom furnished with a bed, a desk and some chairs, a chest, a table, and a television set. The foyer also leads to a kitchen, which has a full wall of cabinets and work space including sink, a full-size refrigerator, and a good-size stove. Remarkably serene and well-functioning, Mrs. T. says she has three hours of home help cleaning service a week but supplements it herself. The place sparkles—like everywhere else in this building and in Öster-gården. Furniture is highly polished; pictures are dusted and well displayed; there are doilies. Silver pieces and trophies are well polished. People are encouraged to bring favorite pieces of furniture. Mrs. T. told us that she likes living here better than in the central city because she is now free of the hazards of heavy traffic. Her seventy-year-old daughter lives in a nearby service flat, and they meet together daily in hobby work. Out of the window there is interesting activity and pedestrian traffic. In the distance a factory is being completed.

Later we knocked at the door to a two-room flat at the corner of the corridor in another wing. The two women who live here have come out of the hospital after three years. In this kind of semiprotective environment, an old age home integrated into a housing development, they can live in the community. Both are in wheel chairs. Obviously of middle-class background, their good and plentiful furniture enhances their shared living room–sitting room. Both were embroidering as we arrived. They spoke with intelligence and awareness. The second room is a shared bedroom with two carefully selected beds. The kitchen has all the modern equipment that has been invented for the handicapped —cabinets in closets on adjustable shelf mountings which can be reached from a wheel chair, a stove and sinks which can be used the same way. Similarly, the toilet has all the latest equipment. They both spoke of how pleased they were. They get eight tickets a month for trips wherever they want to go on the "handicapped van" or by taxi. This is exclusive of trips to the doctor. The amount of cleaning time assigned in each flat varies with need. Here, since both have been confined to wheel chairs, they have help twice a day, two hours in the morning and one hour in the afternoon, for cleaning, arranging the apartment, and receiving personal help. At night somebody comes from the center and helps them get to bed. In short, we saw here how service for the aged is part of an integrated system.

The resources for the aged in Hallonbergen include an old people's home with 120 places, 127 service flats (which they call "pensioners' flats"), and 10 flats for invalids, all specially designed. The communal facilities are available for all old people in these special apartments or anywhere in the development; comprised of a day center, a restaurant, a cafeteria, and hobby premises, they are situated in a one-story building. In another connecting one-story building is a sheltered workshop, administered by the county, with one hundred places. Each is easily reached from both the old people's home and the blocks of service flats. The center, in fact, joins the two facilities at the first-floor level.

The residents may eat in the restaurant or cook in their individual kitchens. They have access to a reception desk in the day center, where a telephone operator is on duty day and night, and to rooms for foot care and hairdressing, a library, a special gym, and a bathing section with a sauna and swimming pool, all specially equipped for the physiotherapeutic needs of handicapped or old people.

A model alarm system—the Emergency Warning Aid (EWA)—is being tried out in one of the buildings. Alarms are set off electronically if an old or handicapped person changes his usual daily routines and does not "break" certain electrically time-controlled electronic signals. Some of the professionals we spoke to were enthusiastic, but others saw the entire enterprise, or its variants, as excessive; telephone coverage or alarm buttons in each room are more common.

Walking from the old age block, through the center, we arrived at several wings of service flats. As in the old age block, these are specially designed but without as much special equipment. Each small flat —whether with one or two bed-sitting rooms—has a bath or special safety shower, a modified but well-equipped kitchen, and adequate closet and storage space. Most people apparently bring their favorite furniture pieces but special beds are provided. Baths and showers are made readily interchangeable. We learned, in a series of visits, that the population is a working-class–middle-class mix. All the apartments are well maintained, whether by the occupant alone or with home help aid.

The comfortable, modern shopping center just across the way from the facility has a restaurant, open to the public. It is set up to serve as cafeteria for the old age home and service flat blocks, and also to be the school cafeteria. Physical facility, equipment, design, staffing, are all outstanding. Here, then, in one facility, the entire philosophy of the enterprise is enacted daily.

One Swedish informant was worried about an overemphasis upon technology to replace human contacts and a per-unit cost level which could be too high to maintain. The press has wondered whether the scale is not too large and impersonal. But everyone is proud of the effort that is being made to explore new forms of aid, contact, and normalization. For example, Hallonbergen provides "walking assistants" as part of the social services program, to help old people take a stroll or shop. And it gives it all strong financial backing: at present the monthly rent in the old age home and service flats is below the basic pension level and is not related to economic costs. When we inquired about this apparent generosity, we were told, "Old people have a right to this. They worked hard to establish our present society."

Göteborg

We turn to Sweden's second largest city, Göteborg, to see what is developing in a large population center. Here there is a program halfway between the large, very modern, perhaps somewhat impersonal Hallonbergen facilities and the homelike old people's home, Östergården. Backahus is a "service house" (flats and shared central facilities in a "normal" environment), a combination of an open-care old age home and a community center.

While the facility is modern and well equipped, design and scale maintain a comfortable homelike atmosphere. The core is a multipurpose community center for the aged with a variety of resources serving people from all over the community. It has recreational, social, physiotherapeutic, library, and cafeteria facilities as well as hobby rooms. Like almost all new facilities of this type in Sweden, the center is closely connected to flats for old people in a series of blocks, which therefore provide and share certain facilities going beyond mere apartment-hotel living, but are not as all-inclusive and comprehensive as an old age home.

In this instance, to keep old people "near the center of activities," the architect came up with an unusual solution: four wings of low, red wooden "row houses" are built on top of a one-story building at the commercial center of the Hisingen district, called "the Selma Lagerlöf market." A total of ninety-one one-room flats of 226 square feet each are placed in these "wings" and have exits directly to six wind-sheltered roof-top gardens with green plants, flowers, and benches. Each flat has one or two bed-sitting rooms (furnished by the tenant except for convenient, specially constructed beds), a pantry, a risk-free shower. There is a small foyer. Flats, the central facility, and community center rooms are colorfully decorated in rusts, beiges, reds, greens. The matron believes that old people need bright colors, just as children do; she is critical of the usual "hospital white." There is a preoccupation with design, sight-line, convenience for the old and the handicapped. Moreover, the tenants assisted in selecting room textiles.

Fifteen tenants share each terrace of 263 square yards. Here residents live above the bustle in the streets (only pedestrian traffic) but have a street view and can use the elevator to reach the "senior citizen center" and the shopping area with its drugstore, social security office, a pub, many shops, and small church. The street life is active and interesting. Across the field are a school and playgrounds. Backahus is at the heart of a new housing development which opened three years ago in a section that is essentially a shopping center and service facility. As one enters through a corridor on the ground floor, there is a banking and insurance company at the left, and some of the hobby shops can be seen. An attractive entry leads to a flight of steps to the facility itself. There is an information window, and a variety of central services are immediately visible.

There are basically two wings on one floor containing the flats which are rented to old people. Each of the wings has two eating areas for twelve people. The equivalent of a small cafeteria is available to all. Although the residents have small kitchenettes, most of them eat their meals in the facility since the basic cost is included in the rent for residents; outsiders pay $1.25 or $1.60 a day for the excellent food.

This interesting facility dramatizes the range of Sweden's programs. No two places using a given name are exactly alike: service flat, pensioners' hotel, service building, center. These particular service flats are described as "community care." They seem to be halfway between old age home and service flats for completely self-caring retirees. Some community care facilities place special emphasis on the fact that the old people care for themselves, do their own cooking, and are not in "institutional" environments. On the other hand, in this facility, residents are encouraged to have their meals in the cafeteria, and there are rather large numbers of staff and a variety of supportive and aid services. The old people seemed older here, and many of them needed crutches and a variety of special devices. In effect, this would be called an old age home in some places. Yet it is not under overall medical supervision and does not even have a medical wing for people needing ongoing medical care. Tenants who are ill or injured are sent to a hospital; and we were told that, in effect, this seems to minimize the call for medical care even though the facility offers a great deal of therapeutic rehabilitative activity in addition to beauty parlors, hobby shops, foot care, and recreational programs.

Wherever we visited individual flats and rooms—in Backahus or elsewhere—we found that old people seem to like to have familiar things around them, even if they are not always comfortable or are difficult to clean. And everywhere we went the facilities were extraordinarily clean and well kept.

A woman in her eighties described the residence: "Services are excellent here at Backahus. You can get your meals served. You do not have to clean. You have a garden just outside your door. You do not feel lonely. You are near to everything around—even to the kindergarten, if you want to be with children. You can get services whenever you need. You just press one of these buttons, see . . . ," and she showed us the signal buttons placed at strategic points in the flat, at the bedside, in the bathroom, in the kitchenette.

This lady lived previously in an old "poor" district in inner Göteborg. She is a widow, and her children have their own families to care for and can help her only now and then. When she began to have heart trouble, she did not dare to stay alone in her flat at night. She does not actually need constant medical care, but she wants to be in a safe place, where she can call for someone in case of need: "This is the ideal solution. An old person cannot wish for a better place to spend her old days," she said, pointing to the pleasant view over the flowers on the terrace just outside the glassed door of her flat.

She rents this flat by a contract with the social administration of Göteborg. She can come and go as she pleases, just as if she rented a flat in an ordinary house. The difference is the immediate access to services and protection day and night, and to meals, if she wishes.

Her only income is the basic old-age pension and she therefore has a municipal housing allowance for the rent. Her fee for food and other services is calculated so that she and others in a similar financial situation will always have 30 percent of their pension income left for pocket money. Each flat of twenty-five square yards costs $1,375 in annual rent—higher than ordinary flats with similar space, but low considering the extra advantages of living safely. Municipal means-tested housing allowances enable pensioners to pay these rates.

Göteborg has a population of 70,000 over age seventy in a general population of some 600,000. It now has 300 service flats in special service houses of this sort, plus 200 other flats for old people scattered in regular housing. There are 250 geriatric beds in a special hospital and elsewhere. Some 14,000 retirees or handicapped people get home help services. About 350 get meals-on-wheels delivery. While the belief is that congregate eating—in center cafeterias and schools—is better for most old people, the social welfare authorities know that many people are geographically isolated. They therefore are now experimenting with delivering not only meals but also grocery orders so that people can do their own shopping by phone if they live too far away to walk to the shops.

The service flats have alarm systems—usually a button in each room. For other old people in the community, there is a nighttime emergency standby service which serves all community medical and related emergencies. This social service department provides access to three experienced nurses who are hooked into the police department emergency number to serve the aged along with others. There are ten to twelve calls a night, with as many as five or six hundred in June and July of 1973. Many calls report psychiatric emergencies or problems in other than aged families, of course.

With two thousand people on waiting lists (far longer than any such lists we encountered elsewhere in Sweden), the average age at admission is eighty. Most of the residents in the regular flats and the flats in service buildings appear remarkably self-sufficient and able to cope. But many others need a measure of protection and help with strenuous activity, or even with daily routine.

Göteborg also illustrates a degree of inventiveness in community centers for the aged. Not all are tied to new residential arrangements.

Thus, in a run-down area we visited an abandoned library, originally set up by private philanthropy, which had been a community center but had declined. It had been "seized" by a radical group of squatters for a while. Then it was cleaned up and made into a morning and afternoon center for the aged. It is run by two serious and interesting young men. The old Victorian-type library building has been "opened up." There are rooms for a café, one for chess, a room for table tennis and dances, and a variety of other facilities. There is practically no budget and very little equipment, but the staff have created an accepting and attractive atmosphere in a deteriorated, dilapidated building for the more energetic and self-sufficient "aged," to whom it caters.

Göteborg is generous to its aged. Residents of Backahus pay in 70 percent of their full pension and keep about forty-three dollars for personal expenses monthly (with meals covered and medical costs met).[4] The top payment, for people with supplementary pensions and other personal income, is well below the daily economic cost of operations of about eighteen dollars per day. In fact, the average *monthly* per capita payment is twenty-seven dollars. Yet these are self-respecting middle-class and working-class aged, not an underclass or poverty group; there is no sense of charity or stigma, no feeling that one's living standard must decline in retirement. The issue is security, care, amenity; and the community of the aged is socially and economically integrated—both within itself and in the interesting and comfortable environment in which it is placed.

Such big-city facilities are not unique to Göteborg. In a new pensioners' hotel in Stockholm—larger, more conventional in outward appearance, extremely well designed, and expensively equipped—residents come and go as they wish and control the door locks on their apartments, which they rent. The philosophy is similar to that in Göteborg, and we were impressed with the fact that most residents are in their late seventies and eighties. They enjoy the physical aids: low cabinets, special beds, special bathrooms, handrails along the corridors, elevators and doorways which can take wheel chairs. Even more than in Göteborg there is a sense of people with their own rented apartments and personal furnishings. The facility is rich in specialized resources for residents and local aged: dining arrangements, foot care, gym, hydrotherapy, clinic, reading and game rooms, social centers. There

---

4. This is not very different from the U.S. mandated policy on expense money retention for social security retirees in nursing homes, a policy said to need closer monitoring because of frequent abuse.

is, however, no assumption that everyone must use these facilities, and many residents are more oriented outside the hotel. There is coming and going. Some of the old people eat in a school across the way which serves them subsidized meals following the children's noontime meal.

One has the impression that the service flats in regular housing, service hotels, or service buildings, or in old age homes, differ in the degree of self-sufficiency and facility-dependency of their residents. There is a great variation in the amount of and need for medical care —and the view of the appropriateness of having special long-term or short-term infirmaries in community living arrangements. Each municipality seems to be making its own "boundary" decisions and experimenting with linkages between the medical and the social.

And residents who cluster into each of the facilities adjust to (and perhaps are self-selective with regard to) the local policies. In the Stockholm facility, as in Göteborg, we met interested, satisfied consumers. They are reading, looking at activity outside, walking, napping, participating in hobby work or therapy. The depressed atmosphere of many American facilities is not visible.

Orebro

Located in the center of the country, the industrial city of Örebro has a population of 115,000, of whom 13 percent are over retirement age. It offers a spectacular "new town" plan which groups 1,800 apartments (for 5,500 people) around a well-equipped service center which includes a school. Brickebacken, which opened in 1970, takes "integration" another step forward: communal facilities are built so as to meet the special needs of various groups, while enriching resources for everyone. Recreation, cultural activity, and education are maximized for all. Yet the basic stress is on community. In this environment the elderly do not need to feel lonely or pushed around, yet they can also get away into a protected setting if they wish.

One notices immediately upon approaching Brickebacken that there is something special about this place. Most of the dwellings are two-story, rather long, garden apartment buildings, interestingly placed in relation to hill and land contours. There are some three-level buildings. In the center, beyond a parking lot, one sees a very attractive "service" center. What is most remarkable as one approaches is the color everywhere. At the entrance to the service area, past a shopping unit, there is a walk with facilities on both sides. To the left, in front of the service center, is a schoolyard. To the right are food shops and a restaurant which serves the school, old people, and the public at large. Inside the service center, opposite the restaurant, are the several types of public health facilities which the town provides—public health nurse, dentist, well-baby clinic. To the left of the entrance, along a much longer corridor, past colored benches, rock garden areas, and a variety of doors, are the library and schoolrooms (on both sides of the corridor). One sees several types of classrooms, shops, textile classes, music rooms. All the facilities are used for community purposes after school hours; some are shared during the school day. Thus, people building a boat, for instance, may rent space and use tools and storage space in the woodwork shop. There are also club rooms, a large gymnasium, and a swimming pool. After school this is a general, well-equipped, community facility.

At midday a number of elderly people were using the library reading room and music room; schoolchildren were in the library. Several of the "senior citizens" were watching the interesting corridor traffic through the glass walls. Others were in the cafeteria. They reach the medical, eating, library, and recreational facilities by walking along covered galleries which connect the service center to the two six-story apartment buildings in which there are special flats for old people.

Brickebacken admitted its first tenants in 1970. By now the area contains 1,800 flats in eighty-two two-story buildings, nine three-story buildings, and nine six-story buildings, all in brick and painted in warm colors, surrounded by naturally contoured landscape.

Some seventy flats for the elderly are located in the two six-story buildings at the service center. Elderly residents in these buildings also have access to extra "communal" three-room flats with kitchens, in each house. These serve as meeting places for the elderly, for club activities, for study circles, for an evening cup of tea together, or just for looking at television programs in company.

The apartments for the elderly have signal buttons at strategic points, connected to the small office of the "service hostess" on duty. There is one such office in each building with special flats. Staff are supplied by the communal social welfare program.

"Do you like living here?" we asked Mrs. E. E., a lively lady well over seventy, who is a former waitress and one of the first residents at Brickebacken. "You bet I do," she responded at once and with conviction. "Just look at my flat: my two big rooms and the balconies outside my kitchen and my bedroom with a passage between them. There I have my private 'garden.' In summertime I plant lots of flowers —my hobby from the old days. Outside the balcony I have all those bushes, trees, flowers, stones in our atrium yard, landscape to look at. You see, I have a long bench here, where I can lie on my balcony-garden, feet propped on the rail. When I first put them there the dentist opposite shook his fist and said, 'Old ladies should not behave like that.' I just shook back and laughed. No, it is really pleasant here—fine neighbors and so green and beautiful around. I can sit for hours and watch the children playing in the yard below. If it is cold I sit in my kitchen. You see, I have a good place for my dining table here in a very modern kitchen."

Mrs. E. E. showed us her furniture and equipment with pride. The rooms are actually quite small, in the style of all these flats, as is the "balcony," but it is all adequate and easy to maintain. Brickebacken has fifty-one more such two-room flats, each 523 square feet, twelve less popular one-room flats (371 square feet), and six three-room flats (910 square feet). The respective rents are $97, $76, and $148, rates which are below economic costs and which (as everywhere in Sweden) are paid by most residents through a combination of their own pensions and municipal housing allowances.

Beds, cabinets, sinks, closets, doorways are obviously engineered with knowledge of the needs of older people. The bathtub can be lifted out easily and replaced by a shower, if the resident prefers it. It can as easily be shifted back, if a new tenant prefers the bathtub. For old people who prefer to have showers in their flats but temporarily want a tub bath, there is a bathroom in the building, equipped with all necessary technical aids for easy lifting, and the service staff or home care attendants will help with the bath.

The staff is on duty until 10:00 in the evening, ready to help if someone calls for a service. At night the alarm system is connected to a central alarm office, which also is responsible for other service flats in town catering to the elderly and handicapped. "Is the night alarm often used?" we asked. The answer was a surprise: only five times since 1972. However, some old people telephone at night in order to have someone to talk to. Their calls are received by a home care attendant on duty. During the day, many of the older tenants use their alarm buttons to call for services. But at night the alarm is reserved for emergencies. The hostess on daytime duty calls those pensioners who require a daily check.

Örebro has recently tried more modest-sized solutions in building for the elderly. In the outskirts of the central part of town a service house and an old people's home have been built in combination with a day center, which also serves all elderly people living close to it in these older parts of the town. This center in Södermalmshemmet (South-end Home) is situated at walking distance—766 yards—from the former central market (Stortorget).

In Södermalmshemmet, 144 retirees live in the old people's home, situated in two six-story buildings, and 59 live in service flats in a five-story building. Here, too, a day center in the basement building joins the three houses.

The staff consists of eighty persons, employed part- or full-time. The day center has a restaurant, with meals at reduced prices for pensioners (ninety cents for a hot meal) and the usual hobby and service facilities observed in all new centers: craft shops, reading room, foot care, beauty parlor, rooms for medical checkups, physiotherapy, sauna, and water supply. Everything here has a homelike, friendly appearance.

In the old people's home, too, residents use their own furniture except for the bed. Rooms have a lavatory and a hot plate. In Södermalmshemmet there is also a shower close to each room—by no means the universal situation in what are called old people's homes.

In his sunny, pleasant-looking room of 140 square feet we met Oskar K., eighty-eight years old and formerly a low-ranking railway employee. He has lived here for three years and is very pleased with his room. His neighbor, Mrs. P., eighty-six years old, offered to make a cup of coffee in her pantry: "I do it every day for myself or for a guest and am so glad I have this opportunity to cook on a hot plate, although we get all meals we need. I also like that we only live twelve on each flat [wing]. It is more family-like this way." Their standard of food, clothing, and furniture appears to be better than that of people of similar station in the United States.

The retired old people living in the old people's home need considerable service, particularly light medical care, and get it regularly through the service staff. The services also may be used by retirees living in the service flats in the other house, but they must pay for them, whereas the services "go with" the old age home fee.

The old people's home and the day center are rented by the owner, the municipal cooperative housing estate foundation, to the social welfare committee of the town. But all service house tenants have their own contracts directly with the foundation and pay rent to it. They can live quite independently here, if they prefer to. The use of services and ties to the day center are voluntary. People feel and act like hotel residents, not like institutionalized invalids.

The town and municipality of Örebro now has 14 old people's homes for about one thousand retirees and 243 service flats for three hundred. For other old people, living in their homes, Örebro also has rapidly expanded its home help services.

Telephones, Meals, and Other Supports

Clearly service houses, "pensioners' hotels," old age homes, service flats are all expressions of a more basic concept: they are part of the "community support" or "environmental support" system which avoids unneeded hospitalization, increases security, and stresses "normalization." Thus there is reciprocal relationship among the home help–home health programs and these facilities, including the living arrangements and the day centers. Congregate eating arrangements and meals-on-wheels have already been mentioned, as have the "walking assistants." Telephone services and food shopping arrangements deserve at least brief description, since they, too, are part of the support system.

Örebro is one of the first large towns in Sweden to introduce a central telephone and alarm service which old people may call at night. The first municipality to open such a system was Kristianstad, a town in southern Sweden. In 1969 the town advertised in the local press, asking all interested senior citizens to get in touch with the local welfare committee if they wanted daily calls. A home care attendant, responsible for the telephone service, visits each elderly applicant, notes names of relatives and neighbors, and gets an extra key to the flat. The key is kept under lock in the office from which calls are made. The attendant keeps cards on all participants and notes planned absences for hospital stays, holidays, trips, and so on.

Each home care attendant calls all her assigned retirees daily between 8 and 10 A.M. Every second weekend she is replaced by another home help attendant to allow time off. The calls are generally very short, just to check that everything is all right. If one of the old people does not answer, the caller contacts the neighbor or relative who lives nearest. If they cannot find out why the old person does not answer, the home help makes a home visit, using the extra key. If needed, she contacts a district nurse, a doctor, or a hospital.

If the old person reports not feeling well, the home help makes a home visit or calls the district nurse. Experience from this activity, now spread to other municipalities, shows that old people feel more secure given such daily telephone checks. The home help is usually employed by the social welfare committee and paid by the hour for time spent on calls and home visits. The service is in the home help category.

Kristianstad has gone from one to three telephone checkers as demand for the service has increased. At least one life has been saved. Officials believe that early discovery cuts more expensive medical and hospital costs. In any case, loneliness is alleviated.

Telephone service may be possible for rural areas and small towns too small for old people's homes or specialized blocks of service flats with alarm systems. Thus, in Nyköping, forty old people in their own homes can count on a telephone call at a time they specify. Many seem to want to be called at holiday time, when relatives and friends are away. The telephone callers are employed by the social welfare committee. They often help elderly people to find telephone numbers or addresses they cannot easily find themselves—and which they need.

Stockholm has not yet organized for telephone checks, but plans are under way. First, alarm systems in old age homes and pensioners' flats will be wired into a central location for nighttime emergency coverage. Then the number will be given out for direct calls by old people living alone in ordinary apartments. Finally, the central facility will take on the "checkup" calls. In the meantime the pensioners' federation is campaigning for free telephone service for pensioners. The phone coverage rate in Sweden is very high but there are some old people who lack phones. As in England and the United States, where there is a similar movement and conviction that access to phones copes with loneliness and saves lives in emergencies, the investment is considered modest and very worthwhile.

An additional word also must be said about the experimental "meals-on-wheels" services being tried out in several municipalities. Some have had good results, especially those where home care attendants, service patrols, or the mailman brings food from a school kitchen in sparsely populated areas. But these are not rapidly expanding services. There seems to be a certain resistance among the elderly against ready-made food of a kind they are not used to. Old people do not easily change their eating habits. Many prefer to have a home help come and cook, or to cook themselves from frozen or fresh food brought by home helps or others.

In big cities like Stockholm old people can also order food sent from nearby shops. The delivery charge is paid by the municipality, when needed. Five times a month elderly persons in Stockholm who have applied for this type of service have the right to send for food delivery. The social welfare committee pays back forty-five cents of the delivery charge if it is sixty-eight cents (the usual price), twenty-three if the fee is forty-five to sixty-eight cents; if the fee is lower, the old person must pay the whole cost.

The home care attendant also may help with shopping—especially for people over ninety years of age. If old people prefer to go to the shops themselves and see the food, the home care attendant may accompany them, taking them for a walk at the same time. The retiree also may walk alone to the shop, buy a weekly supply of groceries, and have the things sent. The bill for delivery goes to the social welfare committee.

Day centers run apart from old people's homes and service flats are also expanding as a solution to the meal and loneliness problems and as a locus for specialized services for the aged. Of the fifty day centers built in Sweden in recent years, half are independent of residential facilities.

Most of the day centers are open five days a week, some also on Saturdays and Sundays. Hours are generally 9 A.M. to 4 P.M. Members have keys to some of the centers and can use the facilities even when they are closed and without staff. Apart from meals the most common services offered in these centers are gymnastics and pedicare (half of the centers). Hairdressing and bath services are also given in about one-third of all centers. Almost all centers offer hobby and handicraft activities, with a more or less rich variety. Half offer study circles and courses for older persons.

Debate

Municipalities do the specific planning for the aged in Sweden—in a context of overall national leadership, supports, and policy. It is therefore not surprising that each seems to have a somewhat unique delineation of what is the province of the medical facilities, what belongs to the old age homes (pensioners' hotels), what is the domain of service houses or service flats, and what is community care for those who remain in their own homes or apartments. Each draws in its own way upon central governmental construction and operational subsidies and decides the extent to which national program initiatives (and even directional pressures via subsidy) will be followed. Because municipalities control considerable revenue through their own income taxes, their initiatives are important. Each also sets its housing allowance levels for retirees.

Malmö, the final city we selected, is a place where one may visit an extraordinarily attractive "integrated" facility for the aged. Malmö sees advantages in a diversity of resources in one center, even a center for the aged alone, as long as it is not geographically hidden away from the city at large. "Old age home" rooms and service flats can be in one building provided the former are closest to shared facilities. The director of the social welfare service has written:

The immediate five-year plan for Malmö provides for five centres in five different parts of the town. Each centre will contain an old people's home, a pensioners' home, and a community centre for daily use. The intention is to provide qualified specific care for the aged both for those who reside there and for a large number of pensioners who reside in that part of town, for whom an effective stimulating care including preventive medicine would be of great medical and psychological importance. Furthermore, we believe that the daily care will provide a valuable link between the open and the closed social care of the aged, a form of intermediary care which ultimately can erase the old picture of institutional treatment.

This policy has been translated into beautifully designed and executed buildings, landscaping, outdoor theater, pubs, community centers, sheltered gardens, outdoor pool, cafeterias, and all the usual services, shops, and resources which one associates with daily living for people over seventy.

Social policy is serious business in Sweden, the center of domestic politics. And old people constitute a major, potent voting bloc. Beyond this the society obviously has real commitment to offering a decent life to its aged. Not surprisingly, therefore, the elderly in Sweden already command a significantly large share of the total national health and welfare budget.

A recent survey reports that on the average the municipalities spend about seven times more for the care of the elderly than for children of preschool age. In general, services to the elderly take about 10 percent of the municipal budget, whereas day nurseries, nursery schools, and other "open care" arrangements for children cost municipalities about 1.4 percent of their budgets.

In the field of services to the aged there is a recognized obligation to search out those with needs and to offer service. The data suggest that Sweden does a good deal—and pays a large price. (Not that it is unusual in modern industrial countries to invest more in services to the aged than in those for children; among other things, the types of services needed by old people are more costly.) Despite what may seem to outsiders a generous and considerate approach, in Sweden there are constant complaints. Many want major improvements.

For example, active leaders in the National Federation of Swedish Pensioners (PRO) want to take over the responsibility for leisure time activities and study circles in the day centers. They are not always content with the sort of "entertainment for the elderly" now offered. On the other hand there has not yet developed a movement for full control by the elderly of services organized in their behalf. Pensioners, after all, are adequate people, defined as such and often completely capable and self-sufficient physically.

Journalists and critics continue to remind Sweden that despite progress and many excellent benefits and facilities, it has much unfinished business in this field. Many old and handicapped people are said to be isolated in the community or miserable in old-style impersonal institutions. The society owes them something better "in solidarity" with the generation which moved the country from poverty and backwardness to its current prosperity and its welfare state institutions.

There is a response by government and people at large. The policy, as indicated, is "normalization." At the start of 1972, Sweden had 543 service houses and 5,439 service flats of the kinds here described. Because 60,000 elderly are still in old people's homes, efforts are being made to modernize and improve them, to make them somewhat more open. Only the chronically ill aged in need of constant care are believed to require nursing homes and hospitalization ("long-term clinics"). These are the oldest among the retired, generally people over eighty-five. Over 43,000 beds were so assigned in 1970. But emphasis is on the service flats located in service houses, in blocks in new housing, or as flats scattered among apartments for families. And even service flats are not used if physical renovation of the person's home or apartment will do. Thus there is a generous loan program to permit building renovation to accommodate the daily living needs of old people; interest rates are means-tested and very low.

Although the pace of service flat construction has slowed, because of financial constraints, from four thousand units a year in the 1960s to one thousand a year in the early 1970s, commitment has not lessened. The retiree population is growing at a rate of 20,000 annually, and there is clear evidence of intent to do more as resources permit. The facilities we have described are outstanding or at least better than average; they are to be the norm. If the building pace cannot be speeded at a given moment, at least a larger investment in home helps and similar services will strengthen community care resources.

Such an approach fits what to a visitor emerges as a developing strategy: For most people the first postretirement period will be one of "regular" community living, supported by pensions, general health services, congregate meals, home helps, community centers for the aged. Then, in the mid or late seventies, the service houses and service flats come into use; people living at home will increasingly need more intensive home help service, telephone checks, shopping aid, meal services. Old age homes, to be called pensioners' hotels, will usually be for people over eighty-five needing more protective environments and access to more medical support. Nursing homes, clinics, hospitals will take over when and where medical care is the predominant need. In short, the program recognizes that "old people" are several groups; they need differentiated programs.

The capacity to function is more important than specific age, of course, and old people responded to a major Swedish survey by choosing among ordinary flat, service house or flat, or old age home (pensioners' hotel) according to whether they were "physically fit and mobile," "often sickly, less mobile," or "always sickly and/or unable to move without help." Those needing full medical supervision belong elsewhere. Current planning reports, especially for residential care, do distinguish among those under seventy, under seventy-five, under eighty, under eighty-five, under ninety, since the ages are partially predictive of rates of functional incapacity. Each of the cohorts is growing and the dividing line between nonresidential facilities for the aged is gradually moving upward. Planners assume at present that about 6 percent of the aged over seventy may need service flats and rooms in old age homes, 5 percent may need nursing home–hospital accommodations (generally county operated), and the rest can be sustained in their own homes by supportive social services.

All the Swedish efforts are premised on the general pension system (a basic pension for all plus an earnings-related supplement) and excellent health and hospital protection. Without these, all efforts to create supportive environments for the aged would come to naught. Nor would the system work without the generous means-tested, non-stigmatic housing allowances drawn upon by 80 percent of all retirees, or without the eating, transportation, home help, and community center resources.

There are clashes, debates, differences—but a considerable moral consensus. Sweden, at least, thinks of old age as an honorable status. Social invention can make it more pleasant for all.

"You Can't Do This . . ."

The retirement movement in the United States has generated spectacular, comfortable facilities for those who can afford them, though often more age-segregated than the experts might recommend. But why not leave that to preference: some retirees apparently like retirement villages, whether for safety, companionship, or for the recreation facilities. The less affluent may live in trailer camps, some attractive and adequate, others marginal and shameful. Larger percentages of the aged continue to live alone in their home communities, or with children and relatives. If widowed or widowered, they try to manage their apartments and homes, but may have to resort to rooming houses and declining hotels.

Data on provision are decentralized to states and localities, and program definitions and boundaries are inconsistent. Thus exact statistical comparisons with Sweden are not possible. However, one number tells the story: the 1970 White House Conference on Aging found that six million older Americans live in unsatisfactory housing. All housing for the elderly subsidized by the Department of Housing and Urban Development to date adds up to something under 400,000 units.

The U.S. public subsidy program assures a fixed percentage of units for the aged and the handicapped. It offers apartment and house renovation loans. It backs special housing units—like service houses—and includes provision for community facilities. But planning and programing are fragmented, compete with other priorities, and consider their targets to be the poorer, less fortunate aged. As such the provision never seems to be of a scale, quality, or scope to match needs.

Similarly, we have community care and support systems of all sorts, but at local initiative, on a small scale, and with no serious attempts at coverage.

Here, then, is the difference. Sweden, small, homogeneous, and affluent, is not to be compared with the United States, but it holds a lesson. It assumes that the status of old age calls for supportive services for those who remain in their homes and for community care and living arrangements for members of all economic groups, and as a natural, normal service, for which there is no apology. In the United States we have neither recognized the need nor accepted the responsibility.

Sweden has also seen the wisdom of facility continuity (from own apartment, to semiprotected flat, to service house, to facility with medical resources, to medical facility)—not all of this for any one person, but the range needed for the range of needs. So have we. But except for the occasional experimental project or outstanding program, we have no vehicle for large-scale implementation. We rush tens of thousands of retirees into expensive and often horrible nursing home facilities long before it is necessary.

There is gradual movement in the United States. Social insurance levels are improving and are now keyed to the price index. Supplementary Security Income offers a guarantee to those with inadequate income after retirement. Our health programs for the aged are improving and are on the national agenda. In the housing and community care domain, most of what is described in this report on Sweden have some American counterparts. Yet little that is attractive in the American system and is available to average people exists on a significant scale. What the Swedes would settle upon as a standard for any retiree remains an exception here. "Normalization" is a policy in Stockholm and only an attractive proposal in Washington.

We return, for a final comment, to Södermalmshemmet in Örebro, to a service flat occupied by Mr. and Mrs. R. Their two miniature rooms, a bedroom and a living room, are entered from a foyer. The kitchen is ingeniously laid out, facing the front, and has good window space. There is adequate storage and a well-designed bathroom. The R.'s have brought a careful selection of their possessions with them, so this apartment is beautifully and spotlessly furnished and maintained. It reflects a long life, family ties, fifty years of service in a shoe factory, including a stint as foreman in Massachusetts for the husband, now ninety. The couple communicated with us in English. The woman claims she is eighty-four, but seems younger. She is full of pep and energy and manages to keep this small apartment sparkling without any help at all (except for calling somebody to put up curtains, to reach something that is high up, or the like). Everything is comfortable. Only the bedroom seems cramped for two people. (Others have used the same facilities successfully by simply placing one bed in each of the rooms and making each a bedroom-sitting room, with the possibility of closing a door in between if one wants rest.) Mrs. R. tells us that she cooks when she likes. She can get an escort if she wants to shop in the neighborhood. If they do not want to cook or shop, they can eat in the cafeteria, which is quite cheap. Mrs. R. talks at length about the apartment, with which she is very pleased. Then she thinks about her American experience and turns to the visitor: "You can't do this in the United States. You are too big, too large, and have too many kinds of people."

One wonders.

8

Foundation Blocks

WE have organized the preceding seven chapters as though each service could stand alone: health visitor, day care, school meals; or service flats, homemakers, rent subsidies. But the descriptions have told another story. While social policy is not quite indivisible, its components are generally extremely interdependent. Social services build upon and reinforce one another. They hardly seem viable unless they are developed upon necessary foundations and with essential linkages.

The pensioners' hotels and service flats are not conceivable unless there are homemakers and meal arrangements, as well as subsidized rents. Day care requires a backdrop of child health provision. School meals and health visitors set the necessary level for family allowances, which, in turn, define the levels of unemployment insurance and other income maintenance.

We are particularly impressed—in relation to all these European programs—that their essential point of departure cannot and should not be ignored: *a viable income maintenance level; basic health provision; access to adequate housing.* These countries are not without problems or gaps in their social services, but government is expected to play a central role in creating both a cushion of security against predictable hazard and adequate provision in these fields. And the programs are meant to be good enough for any citizen. In the language of social policy they are "universal," not "selective"—for all people, not just for the poor.

We do not here offer specific detailed descriptions of social insurance or of general health services because there is considerable public discussion of alternatives in the United States, and the European programs are outlined and described in readily available sources. It should be noted, however, that in addition to social insurance and supplementary benefit programs similar to ours, each of these countries has a significant family allowance program. In fact, all major industrial countries except the United States, sixty-two in all, have such programs. Grants are automatically paid on a monthly basis to contribute to the costs of child rearing. The variations among countries have to do with grant level, whether or not all children in a family are eligible, the tax status of the grant, whether there is any sort of an income test. Nobody questions the need for a money floor below child rearing. The allowances do not create higher birth rates. They are valued wherever they exist and are especially significant to the poor, to the working class, and to post-secondary students (to whom the grants are paid directly).

Health programs vary, too, from the national health service—which involves a unified system largely devoid of market elements—to a system in which either general physicians and specialists or hospital services remain free enterprise services, despite considerable regulation and payment out of insurance funds. In any case, except for the very affluent, some of whom prefer completely private service, the populations of all these countries are assured of basic doctor and hospital coverage as a right at reasonable cost and not segregated by income level. Their children enjoy regular checkups and preventive service at least during the first few years of life.

We may draw illustrations from two of the countries we surveyed: Sweden and England.[1] Sweden bases its health system on county and municipal government ownership of general hospitals. These units build, maintain, and operate hospitals. The specialists are salaried members of their staffs. Everybody must be covered by government-sponsored health insurance. General practitioners provide care only outside the hospital and refer to specialists on the hospital staffs. General practitioners are paid fees for service, and health insurance refunds about 75 percent of a patient's costs. Norms set by professional associations govern fee schedules. Drugs are included among the benefits covered by health insurance; except in the instance of life-saving drugs, the patient pays half the costs. About 85 percent of all costs are met by governmental sources or from such obligatory sources as payroll deductions.

In England, by contrast, universal coverage is assured by giving everyone the right to sign up with a general practitioner. Doctors are

1. This summary follows closely the overview in Oden W. Anderson, *Health Care: Can There Be Equality?* (New York: John Wiley & Sons, 1972).

paid on a capitation basis arrived at through bargaining negotiations between governmental officials and representatives of the physicians. The latter, who rent or own their office space, work alone or in self-organized groups. There are small charges for prescription drugs. The government owns and operates practically all hospitals. While there are small payroll deductions, almost the entire British system is paid for through general revenue funds collected by central government. Private health insurance is a supplement or an alternative for a minority.

Housing coverage is also defined as urgent in all our countries. Government relies less on the market to assure the supply than we do in the United States. For example, local government constructs and rents out housing at a very high rate in England. In Sweden, new town development is initiated, guided, and controlled by central government. Land is controlled and made available for new towns only if the building societies submit forward-looking, integrated plans. Moreover, new town construction is based on prior development of mass transportation. Yet there are no ideal solutions as yet in this field and the search continues. Shortages are felt everywhere. Economic realities create community designs, building sizes, and locational patterns which often result in isolation, loneliness, anomie. Adequate social service planning in connection with new town development is rare. The successful ideas and attractive patterns are of interest to all.

To round out our picture, then, we do not attempt a health or income maintenance overview. Our task is to cover newer ground. We turn, therefore, to two more limited fields in which we undertook technical analyses and field visits: attempts to humanize new housing developments in response to family changes and current needs (Denmark and Sweden), and new income benefits for parents which reflect and seek to promote the drive for equality for women, while assuring care for young children (Sweden). The latter, incorporating some unique policies, will be new to many Americans.

Social Facilities in Housing Developments in Sweden and Denmark

The discussions of day care and community residences for the aged in Sweden have depicted the physical settings. Clearly, much of the attractiveness of such facilities is attributable to good physical facility planning and integration of the facility into an appropriate environmental context.

Sweden, building about 100,000 dwelling units a year in recent years, probably has produced more new housing for its population than any country in Europe. Housing and job assurance has been the foundation of their social policy since World War II. Thus, as already seen, one is everywhere impressed with the large proportion of people in Sweden who live in new buildings in new communities, whether "new towns in town" or entire new communities. Everywhere there are brand new, tastefully designed, multicolor, multiple dwellings, some garden apartments two or three stories high and some high-rise. They often are beautifully spread over a wide landscape of hills and valleys. All avoid streets where possible, giving pedestrians protected walks. They all have small and large shopping centers, and all seem to have assured adequate, attractive, strategically located space for preschool programs, elementary school, centers for the aged (including old age homes, service flats, and community centers), clubs, and youth hostels. The outstanding developments, as we have seen, build gymnasiums, pools, and workshops for school-community sharing. A few even plan on restaurant-cafeteria mixes to serve the general public as well as a school and an old age center.

On one visit we saw a little girl, the recently arrived daughter of a Yugoslavian immigrant worker, being given special instructions by the swimming teacher. It was a community with a relatively large number of Finnish, Greek, and Yugoslavian immigrants. The supplementary service and special programs were taken for granted. Throughout Sweden (but in a very incomplete survey) we found many immigrant groups in housing which, externally, was extremely attractive and indistinguishable from that available to others. (Foreign workers were in great demand for some years and the immigrants now constitute 5 percent of the population.) Thus, there is no problem in these areas in assuring space for essential social services for the most needy groups. Other newly arrived immigrants, concentrated in deteriorated inner-city areas and saving money or sending it home, were more disadvantaged but perhaps relatively less so than their American counterparts.

The feeling about a program is sometimes conveyed by its "housing"—its physical facility and decor—as we note when we compare the appearance of U.S. social security offices with our public assistance offices. In this connection there is interest in what we saw on a visit to a "new town in town" in Göteborg. The high-rise apartments are white and black, the middle-sized buildings of other colors. In the middle of the complex is an enormous shopping area, the center of which is a covered mall, three stories high. As we entered the mall we noted a circular staircase, leading first to one level of stores and then to a second level, which contains offices. A prominent sign proclaims that the upper story is the *Socialbyra*, the Social Welfare Office. While hardly typical, this Social Welfare Office in a covered mall in a beautiful shopping center is not considered inappropriate. The offices in the bureau are attractive, comfortable, well carpeted, dignified.

Elsewhere we have described facilities and programs in the Hallonbergen district of Sundbyberg for old people and for preschool programs. It may be helpful to say a little more about the development in which these attractive resources are located.

Planning for Hallonbergen began in 1966, when the municipality acquired Crown land previously used for military purposes. (Here is the major point of departure—a land policy in which municipalities acquire tracts on a large scale and release it to private interests only in relation to publicly developed land use plans.) The decision was made to plan for what the official literature calls "a child-, family-, and invalid-oriented residential district."

For present purposes we may bypass the careful car park and traffic-flow planning, except to note that concern for open space utilization to create a living environment led to the choice of covered car-parking decks: the first floor of each building opens onto walking areas and yards, the basement onto traffic floors and streets.

Environmentalists and energy conservationists are equally delighted with the planning. We quote a concise summary:

The entire Hallonbergen district as well as a major part of the rest of the municipality area is heated by a district heating plant. The purposeful expansion of and changeover to the district heating network in this municipality contribute to reduced air pollution. Another environment-building effort is the investing by the municipal authorities in garbage suction installations in new residential districts.[2] The Sundbyberg municipality has played a pioneering role in this field and parts of the district have had such an installation in operation since 1965–66, and the Hallonbergen houses are connected to this system as they are completed. This refuse disposal system eliminates the problem of disturbing early morning traffic and garbage truck noise and offers the advantage of closed and hygenic transportation of

2. This fascinating system is now being observed by many visitors. The tenant drops garbage into a conventional chute but an ingenious system of ducts and airstream takes over. The refuse may travel up to 1.5 miles before reaching the silo, from which it is fed into heating plant furnaces.

garb. from the individual home to the incinerating furnaces of the district
he g plant, where the refuse becomes fuel for heating of the house. The
de .ing of walkways in the district also means that in wintertime you get
ri. of disturbing traffic by snow-ploughing and sand-spreading vehicles at
t'ie same time as you eliminate a certain accident risk. Since sand-spreading
is no longer needed, the snow at the sides of walkways and playgrounds
also can be kept cleaner.

Hallonbergen planning includes 2,283 flats in five groupings plus
one block of apartment houses for students and other young people
(200 single-room and 40 twin-room units, plus 110 room-and-kitchen-
ette flats, with a chapel and shared facilities) and an old people's
center (the home for 120 aged, a day center, pensioners' flats for 127,
and a work-therapy workshop). There are also a central facility for
shops, restaurant, underground subway station, municipal and town
offices and functions: junior, intermediate, and high schools; a small-
industry and offices building, with restaurant; and playgrounds and
outdoor recreation spaces. The building groups contain four day-care
centers (day nurseries in the Swedish usage) at ground floor level with
space for 395 plus space for what we would call family day-care units
and a child-parking place near the shopping area. The central building
houses a post office, a bank, a restaurant, and food shop space, and
contains space for a medical center. There are the usual laundry-
dryer centers in the building and recreation, classroom, and meeting
space in each block and in the central building, which also includes a
theater, a library, and space for exhibitions and adult education.

One must visit Hallonbergen to appreciate its attractiveness, comfort, and unity. The cooperativeness in sponsorship and the shared
usage are outlined in this final quotation:

> In projecting the Hallonbergen residential district the municipality has
> tried to realize its intentions to build a complete city district which contains
> not only housing units but also service functions and employment. Also, the
> municipal authorities have striven to achieve extensive coordination and
> joint utilization of different facilities irrespective of who may be the owner—
> the housing corporation or the municipality.
>
> As an example we may mention that the restaurant in the Central Building
> will deliver all food to schools, old people's centre and day-nurseries, that
> the school canteen will be located in the Central Building connecting onto
> the restaurant, that the day centre premises in the old people's centre are
> open to all pensioners in the municipality, etc. This means that double setups
> of kitchen equipment, double premises for gymnastics and athletics, etc. can
> be avoided with resultant savings in installations and operating costs.

Denmark, too, refuses to build housing developments without communal facilities. Influenced by the idea behind the British new towns, Denmark decided to create satellite developments outside Copenhagen, the capital city, that would constitute small independent towns, self-contained with regard to all kinds of services. (The original idea that residence and place of work should be placed within the same neighborhood has never been effectively implemented.)

Perhaps in part because private preference continues to be for individual housing, which is far too expensive and requires too much land to be possible for much of the population, public debate has turned to the issue of providing as positive an environment as possible for people living in multiple-dwelling projects. And, as is often the case in the Scandinavian countries, a combination of public concern and government initiative led to social experimentation and innovative approaches to creating such an environment. Here, too, where private enterprise and individual initiative have taken the lead in the United States and stimulated provision for the more affluent only, in Denmark the creative force has been the government and its accepted role in setting public policy for average families.

About 50,000 housing units are completed annually in Denmark. There are 14,500 rental apartments in multiple-dwelling complexes, while the remainder are individually owned houses, built or bought by the residents themselves. Of the total number of apartments, 12,000 are built and owned by nonprofit building societies and only 2,500 are constructed privately. Since these nonprofit organizations receive substantial financial assistance from the government, there is major opportunity to utilize them as an instrument of community policy.

All Danish building activity, not only the nonprofit portion, is financed through long-term mortgages obtained from traditional mortgage institutions that are nonprofit organizations under public control. However, the nonprofit building societies receive certain specified advantages. For example, they can obtain mortgages to cover up to 95 percent of the value of new construction (in contrast to 80 percent for private enterprise building); they receive interest subsidies; and they are exempt from income taxation.

In return for these advantages, they must meet certain requirements. First, construction, building design, and apartment layouts must satisfy certain prescribed government standards; second, preference in renting apartments must be given to low-income families. In recent years, with the increased cost of construction, rentals in these new housing projects have risen sharply, even though they continue to be set by law at levels which just cover costs. The result has been a decrease in the number of low-income applicants. In order to offset this, rent subsidies have been made available by the government to eligible low-income applicants for housing constructed by these societies. However, once the needs of these applicants are met, or if none who are eligible apply, others may be accepted. For all other applicants also, regardless of income, preference continues to be given to families with young children. In addition, up to 10 percent of the space available in these developments may be set aside for elderly tenants, while other units may be assigned to single youths (see Chapter 4). The result, therefore, is a housing community that includes a varied population: young people, families with children, the aged, and often the handicapped, both low-income and middle-class.

Finally, since the location of these new housing developments depends on the possibility of buying suitable land as well as obtaining areas the municipalities have zoned for this type of housing, the development of these projects has also been subject to the influence of local government. For example, if a municipality owns the land desired as a building site, it may lay down certain conditions with regard to construction and design. Since by law the municipalities are required to provide day-care centers, kindergartens, and housing for the aged (and a portion of their expenditures for these purposes is reimbursed by the central government), a standard requirement imposed on all new multiple-dwelling construction is provision of such facilities.

Thus, as a result of a combination of factors, namely the British influence on town planners, Danish social policy in the field of housing, and public concern with the quality of life and the creation of a benign and supportive social environment to enhance this, a wide range of social facilities has been built and integrated into all recently constructed large-scale housing projects. This has taken place through the cooperative efforts of both national and local governmental authorities, as well as private and semiprivate organizations, a complex, somewhat unique, but apparently successful arrangement.

Tindberg is one of the older Danish housing developments and was the first of several we visited. Begun in 1955, construction extended over a period of time and the final units were not completed until 1966. People moved into the project gradually, over a ten-year period. The demand for services grew gradually, so they were developed without acute pressure and integrated into the project. The three-story buildings are constructed in traditional fashion of tan-colored brick; they blend quietly into the landscape, resembling other, individually owned, middle-class homes in the surrounding area. There is only one main road entering the development, which is located in one of the "dormitory" towns in the environs of Copenhagen, like the majority of the projects visited. Most of the men work in the capital. Transportation to and from the city is by a bus that runs every ten minutes at peak morning and late afternoon hours, and every twenty minutes during the rest of the day.

This project is used by the Danes as a sort of "base-line" illustration of early efforts at such developments, to underscore certain inadequacies and problems which the design of later developments was supposed to correct. For example, physical access to the project is difficult and public transportation is limited. In addition, the original project had only one small shopping center, which was not readily accessible to all the buildings and required extensive walking for some residents. As a consequence, another, centrally located, larger shopping center was constructed in the project about one year ago. Although the two schools are situated in the center of the development in such a way that the children do not have to cross the main thoroughfare, in general, pedestrian walks are poorly designed and open to the weather, and few strollers were seen.

Sixty percent of the overall population in this dormitory community remains in the project during the day (mainly women, children, and older people). Despite all the pointing to problems and inadequacies, an American visitor notes the provision in the plans for a day-care center, a primary school, a high school, a home for the aged, pensioners' flats (studio apartments for the elderly), a number of one-story buildings with specially designed apartments for the physically handicapped, and several playgrounds. We especially admired one adventure playground—a "working" playground, with construction materials and equipment that children can use to build things—and a second one containing a variety of animals (goats, sheep, ponies) for whose care the children are responsible. In addition, there is one building with small studio apartments for young people attending the nearby university (or another neighboring vocational school). These accommodations are for students only and must be vacated by them when they leave school.

Another development we visited is a large, high-rise project including five fifteen-story buildings that provide two-thirds of the dwelling units and ten four-story buildings. The project houses about ten thousand people, the equivalent of a small town in Denmark. It comes closer than Tindberg to the original concept of a "new town" in that there are numerous small-scale industries nearby employing between fifty and one hundred people each, and many of the project's residents are able to work close to home. The heart of this project is a large covered shopping center that includes the usual types of stores (food, clothing, pharmacy, florist) as well as a library for adults, another separate library for children, a spacious, attractive room containing television, movie screen, and projector and small tables and chairs— all under the supervision of an experienced child-care worker—for the use of children left alone while their parents are shopping. Although this room was empty when we visited it in the middle of the morning, when the school-age children were otherwise occupied and the younger ones were in the local day-care center, the service was available as needed; the supervisor explained that the facility was heavily used in the afternoons and on weekends.

The newest housing project we visited, as yet only partly completed, is located in a semirural area about a half hour's journey from Copenhagen. Eventually, it will contain a series of beautifully designed three-story buildings; at the time we visited we saw one building that had been finished about a year earlier, two others that were just recently completed, and several more still in varying stages of construction. The exteriors of the buildings are a sort of orange-rust metal that deepens in color with weathering. They looked enormously attractive against the backdrop of green hills and trees. The basement or ground level of the buildings is used as a garage for the tenants. The first floor of one building included several communal meeting rooms, game rooms (for table tennis and billiards), children's playrooms, and a hobby room. One was a miniature workshop, with power tools; a small sailboat was in the process of construction. In a second building, some of these facilities alternated with semienclosed areas adjacent to the entrance halls of three-apartment units. Tenants are free to decorate these areas as they wish. In several places we saw pictures and posters hung on walls and, in others, painted murals; one youngster was busily putting the finishing touches to his own mural, a fantasy of sun, water, and sky. Another area was furnished with an old oriental rug, an over-stuffed couch, and two big club chairs. All these areas open onto the common corridor running the length of the building, so that the effect was of a series of "front porches" facing an enclosed pedestrian walk, providing an opportunity to socialize with one's neighbors, or observe or talk with people as they pass. As we walked by, one resident was using the area as a sort of extra workshop, doing some carpentry work on a bookcase.

One apartment we visited belonged to a young couple, both of whom were university students, and their two children. The rent for their duplex apartment, including two small bedrooms, a bathroom, and a small terrace on the first floor, and a living room, dining room, kitchen, bedroom and bath, and large terrace on the second floor, was $168 monthly. In similar, privately built housing, the rental would be at least three times as much.

Because of its unusual, rather avant-garde design and its out-of-the-way location, this project tends to attract as tenants a combination of students, artists, academics, and people from the media, as well as a few blue-collar workers. Although the buildings are situated close to one another, high walls around the thickly planted terraces provide privacy on the lower floor, and the second-floor windows on the side with least privacy face north, and have skylights, with panes that can be opened, instead of the conventional type. Even on a gray October day, the light in the booklined living room was clear and beautiful, suggesting an artist's particularly comfortable studio.

There is an active tenant's organization, and several other organized groups in the development; however, the communal meeting rooms are still not heavily used, according to some of the residents. Furthermore, it was obvious that the group of children playing near where construction was proceeding on one of the buildings was much larger than the group playing in the children's game room. Danish children are not unlike their American counterparts. The residents interviewed were all enthusiastic about the project, but acknowledged that there was still only limited use being made of many of the facilities available. None of those interviewed had lived there for more than a few months, and several suggested that time was needed for people to "settle in" and acclimate themselves to a new environment. Furthermore, the "essential" facilities, such as day-care centers, were still not available, and this was of far greater concern to the tenants.

Vaerbro Park is another modern housing development constructed in the late 1960s and planned specifically to provide for a complete range of social facilities, including both commercial and social services. The project is situated about nine miles northwest of Copenhagen, and consists of three eight-story apartment houses, five four-story buildings, a large covered shopping center, schools, and a wide range of other facilities. It functions as a self-contained urban unit. According to a statement put out by the nonprofit building society that is responsible for the development, the intention was to create a residential community offering services and functions ensuring maximum opportunities for social contact in order to "provide for the residents' relaxation and a sense of identity with their place of residence and with co-residents."

The project contains 1,327 apartments and has a population of about four thousand. The shopping and collective service center is centrally located and readily accessible to residents of any building in the development through basement passages or roofed paths. The center itself contains an enclosed and heated shopping street with a wide variety of stores. In addition, off this street are an automatic laundry, a post office, supervised playrooms for children of shoppers, two libraries (one for children and a second for adults), conference rooms, club rooms, and a central receptionist's desk. A doctor, dentist, chiropodist, and midwife also have offices in the center. Furthermore, from this street there is access to a hotel, a nursing home for chronic invalids, and specially designed apartments for the elderly. Providing housing for the elderly in this manner ensures them access to the heart of the community, to shopping and services, and to company. Finally, there is a subsidized, nonprofit, attractive, cafeteria-style restaurant, with excellent food at reasonable prices and seating accommodations for about 250 people. All these facilities are heavily utilized by residents as well as people from the surrounding community. Elsewhere in the project, there are schools, day-care centers, after-school centers, playgrounds, all situated in such a manner that children may proceed from their homes to the facilities without crossing any main thoroughfare. Finally, housing accommodations for young people living on their own are also provided.

Fifteen hundred children live in this project. Although it seemed remarkably well serviced to an American visitor, residents complained that fewer than 20 percent of the children are served by the community's day-care, kindergarten, and organized recreational facilities, and an equivalent number have had to go outside the community to obtain such services. At present, there is substantial pressure by residents and members of the tenant organization to increase provision within the project. A related complaint is that the area provided for parking cars is about seven times as large as that reserved for children's play.

A recent government-sponsored study of the use made of shopping and other types of communal facilities, and the importance of these facilities to the social life and activities of residents, revealed that the shopping center and the libraries were the most heavily utilized, but that club rooms and conference rooms and the open green areas between the buildings received minimal use. The study found that tenants tended to make friends with people living in their own buildings or, even more, around the same entry; friends were made only infrequently through use of the communal facilities. However, in support of the residents' complaints, the report also stated that the club rooms might be used more if they were more adequately furnished and equipped, and that the open green spaces were not conducive to use because they were bare of trees and comfortable places for sitting. Again, it is anticipated that some improvements will be made, just as increased service provision and expanded facilities are being planned.

In general, the populations of the various housing developments we visited ranged between four and ten thousand people. Up to 10 percent of the living space in the projects may be set aside for accommodations for the elderly, and all the housing developments we visited had made such assignment. Generally, there is one building specifically designed to provide small studio apartments for older people who can live on their own, or with a minimum of assistance; or comparable accommodations may be included in a building in which most of the apartments are for average families with children. In addition, another, separate, building usually is designed as a nursing home for the elderly who require more extensive care. Often, some of the facilities for the elderly, such as a senior center, may overlook the play area of a day-care center or kindergarten, providing an opportunity for some shared experience for both the children and the aged.

Similarly, the subsidized restaurants included in some of the projects are designed to serve the residents directly, but are open to others in the neighboring community and may also service the schools, day-care centers, and old people's centers. For the most part, these restaurants tend to be small-scale facilities, provided by the nonprofit organizations sponsoring the project in recognition of the fact that the need for service exists, even though the demand may not be sufficient to support a profit-making commercial facility—and working-class people find commercial restaurants expensive. Dining at home continues to be the preference for most Danes. However, it is recognized that some people live alone and sometimes find it convenient not to prepare a meal for themselves; wives and children may be away for a vacation and the husband, left alone at home, finds it easier not to prepare a meal; unexpected guests arrive, and the availability of a restaurant substitutes for lack of provision at home.

In short, these nonprofit restaurants are an interesting, useful beginning but the scale of usage does not suggest that the Danes—any more than the rest of us—have decided that the new patterns of family life and the participation of large numbers of women in the labor force require more elaborate community eating alternatives.

The Home-Parent Role

In almost all countries, the mother-at-home is at a disadvantage: she gets no retirement pension or unemployment insurance, no tax deductions for work expenses, no health insurance or sickness benefits, no vacation benefits, no maternity leaves. Most societies do not acknowledge the mother as a worker, even though many societies so valued her nurturing role that until recently they discouraged her working outside the home when her children were young. In fact, most modern "liberated" women have been expected to continue their home chores (an average of thirty-four hours weekly according to estimates in the April 1972 *Monthly Labor Review*, Washington), in addition to their newly acquired "paid" work, again on the assumption that these household tasks are hardly true work.[3]

Several modest steps in Sweden are thus of interest. One is a tax system in which the income of husband and wife is treated equally and in which marriage is neither an advantage nor a disadvantage from a tax point of view, and is of equal standing with living together out of wedlock. Another is the several fringe benefits which, while quite modest, begin to recognize the houseparent as worker and to make childbirth less of an economic burden for all families.

These latter benefits are perhaps best seen (in translation) through the eyes of a young Swedish woman, who works and who sees in these developments a further step toward equality. She is in a somewhat unusual situation, since her husband will stay at home to care for their child while she goes back to work. She lives in Göteborg, where she works as a school teacher and her name is Mrs. Lisa Andersson. The family lives in a "row house" near a nursery school and well-baby clinic. She is taking her four-month-old for a checkup:

"Nowadays all babies are automatically registered at well-baby clinics right from their birth. It's done by the hospital or the maternity ward. Like all new mothers I got a house call from the local child-care nurse during my first week at home. Visits to the well-baby clinic are

---

3. A 1973 pamphlet by the Chase Manhattan Bank calculates the average housewife's labor as having a marketplace value of $159.34 for a 99.6 hour week, or $8,285.68 per year.

not compulsory, but regular inoculations are. So most parents use it, just as mothers use the public maternity care.[4] Why pay extra to a private doctor, when public maternity and baby health care is good? And it happens to be here. I have friends, though, living elsewhere, who are less lucky. They sometimes complain of long waiting lines in both well-baby clinics and maternity dispensaries, with little consulting time with a rushed doctor and little chance for talking.

"People at the maternity section of the hospital where Johan was to be born were most friendly, helpful, and attentive, so I fortunately felt well prepared for the delivery. I personally have had good help from the doctor at all the visits before and after the delivery. Both the delivery and the checkups before and after birth are free of charge of course."

Young mothers like Mrs. Andersson have known no other system in their lifetime. They go from monthly to bimonthly visits until the child is a year old (an average of eight visits in the first year), then semiannual checkups and inoculation until school age. After that there are regular school checkups. Not that there are not overcrowded clinics and complaints about service. In some places trained nurses substitute for pediatricians in short supply. However, much of the Swedish system of services for children has as its point of departure the fact that 95–98 percent of all children are checked, free of charge, during the first year of life by public well-baby clinics.

We were impressed with this particular clinic. It is adjacent to a day nursery and the doctor also gives the nursery coverage. We entered a waiting room set up as a miniature indoor adventure playground; while waiting their turns, the children can relax. And doctors and nurses have opportunities for informal observation of the child and of mother-child interaction.

We suspect that only a tradition which produces such coverage can take the next tentative, experimental step enthusiastically outlined by Mrs. Andersson. The discussion resumes when, after the child's checkup, she announces her intention to go back to work. She is asked why so soon, since the child is only four months old. After all, Swedish women have been guaranteed six months' maternity leave for some time:

"Well, you see, for one thing it is not only *my* child, it happens to be *ours*. Both my husband and I believe in children's right to have both

---

4. According to recent statistics 95 percent of pregnant women in Sweden use the public maternity care and free delivery.

a father and a mother present in their lives. We talked this over carefully before getting married. We have decided to try out the brand new 'parent leave,' which permits the father, too, to stay home to care for the baby during its first months.

"We are at least giving the idea a try. Other friends of ours have tried, with more or less success. Letting a young mother stay home in the isolation of a modern suburb with a baby in her charge twenty-four hours round the clock is not a really good solution, anyway. People need a sort of balance in their lives. . . . I feel that I could not stand staying away from my work and my colleagues for a year and a half. Now, had you come next week you might have met my husband here instead of me, taking Johan for checkups or for his daily walk in the baby carriage. My husband looks forward to it. He has even already bought a baby carrier so that he can carry Johan around on his front, 'dialoguing' with him as much as possible from the very beginning. . . . Johan is getting rather heavy now, and my husband is stronger than I, so why not let him have a chance to mind the baby full time?"

We asked how the Anderssons will swing this kind of plan financially:

"First of all we get the basic child allowance, distributed to all Swedish children under sixteen. It has just been increased to about $345 a year, paid quarterly. Every family gets it instead of—as formerly—a tax reduction for dependent children. Had Johan been handicapped physically or mentally we should have been entitled to an extra allowance to take care of him at home. Then the brand new parent leave system and the so-called parent insurance under the national social sickness benefit system will make it workable financially for us. Up to last year all Swedish mothers with newborn children used to get a 'maternity allowance' of about $245, paid at the baby's birth. Working mothers were entitled to six months' maternity leave with their normal sickness benefit slightly reduced, if they had been employed for at least 290 days before the child's birth. Now this is changed: the 'maternity leave' has been prolonged to seven months and transformed to a 'parental leave' in accordance with the new family policy philosophy. So the *father* can choose to stay home and care for the baby for a period, if the parents decide to share the leave.[5] The sickness benefit granted is at a minimum level, under $5.75 a day for the parent staying home. This sum is also paid automatically to homeworking parents

5. Thus far the father take-up remains small.

who are not employed. My neighbor for instance, who has always been a housewife, will get this sum now when caring for her new baby, which will improve their situation considerably.

"Working people's sickness benefit is based on their income level. You get '90 percent' if you choose to stay home to care for a baby. For instance, I earn about $9,300 per year as a teacher. This income entitles me to about $22 a day as a parental sickness benefit—90 percent of my annual income divided by 365. My husband works part time and studies at evening courses at the university at present, so his income is smaller—about $6,800. He will get $16.50 a day when staying home with Johan for the remaining three months. We will lose a bit by this arrangement but the benefit is taxed, so the difference is not great. My husband wants to be with Johan to get to know him. He counts on being able to study more when not having to go to work daily. And I want to go back to work. My neighbor's family, on the other hand, would gain considerably if she took a job now and he stayed home to take care of the children. He has a much higher income—$13,700 per year—and would thus get almost $34 per day. She only gets the minimum sum—$5.75. But they do not want to switch. They are a rather typical Swedish family with traditional attitudes to sex roles. They think we are crazy."

Thus the Swedish houseparent, helped with a cash maternity allowance at childbirth as is the Swedish female worker, now also has a cash benefit during a parent's "leave" after childbirth too. The level is low but the principle innovative. Under the Swedish social insurance system, Swedish houseparents also are paid cash "sickness benefits" as are workers certified as unable to discharge their "work" obligations.[6] Again, the level is low, scaled to what is paid an unskilled worker, but Swedish parents feel that an important principle is established—and the funds are not insignificant.

In the same "package" of measures is the right to up to ten days per year of sickness benefits, to be taken by either parent, to care for a sick child at home. (The average time a child stays home from nursery school is twenty-five days.) While the Swedes are experimenting with special nursery school staff ("child minders") for such cover-

6. About one-third of U.S. wage and salary workers in private industry and government employment are not protected through their place of employment for short-term nonoccupational disability. We, of course, have no cash sickness benefits or any other Social Security coverage for housewives. The current daily sickness benefit for a Swedish houseparent is $1.35 (6 SKR). For a small voluntary premium she can raise her coverage to 15 SKR, about $3.40 at this writing.

age they know that some parents want to stay home themselves—perhaps most do when they are anxious about a child's illness. This policy, of course, raises complex questions.

These are interesting beginnings to respond to the desire to lessen the burden of women's entry into the labor force, while upgrading the houseparent role and promoting a new kind of parental role-sharing in the context of equality.[7] Sweden also offers young couples, on a means-tested basis, long-term, low-interest loans to furnish apartments. Unmarried mothers and fathers are also eligible. Take-up is not large.

An American Connection?

The United States has several outstanding new towns and some public and private housing developments that have concerned themselves about amenity, quality of life, and services. But our national housing policy is far behind in meeting widely accepted building targets, and our program failures lead to a division of interest between subsidizing tenants and purchasers on the one hand, and land clearance, builders, and landlords on the other. Community facility and infrastructure subsidy are also accepted as necessities. Our leading architects and urban designers are not without proposals in the domain of community amenity and a group of environmental psychologists are interesting, even convincing. However, their leads are not yet widely followed. We have a long way to go, whether in new towns or in large-scale publicly operated or publicly subsidized housing in existing communities, in seizing the opportunity for improving the quality of daily life. Daily living can be beneficially affected in the various stages of the life cycle by design decisions and provision of proper services.

In the income security field, an American debate has begun about the viability of the houseparent role as an option for those who want to rear children. Houseparent wages and related social insurance benefits are being proposed. No immediate legislative response is apparent.

7. Perhaps a Swedish critique of this type of formulation will express the perspective of those who have given leadership to these reforms: "This is not quite correct. It is not a question of lessening the burden of female *entry.* . . . Women in Sweden, as in most other countries, always were in the labor force—but in the unpaid sections: family agriculture, trade, handicraft, home textile industry, nurturing professions (child nurses, sick nurses, old peoples' nurses), etc. It is rather a matter of now recognizing domestic work as part of the gross national product and of upgrading the role of parents of small children who care for them at home. Also of facilitating the sharing of the housewife role by both parents."

Indeed, few have as yet joined the discussion. Higher on the reform agenda are a series of social insurance reforms to wipe out the second-class status of the employed married woman (whose social insurance status is that of wife, if married and not at a high income level, and who is not much better off than if out of the labor force). There is no evidence of initiatives to help young couples get started with household and family formation. Family allowances, supported by a minority of experts, are advocated but bypassed for means-tested programs aimed at the poorest and "efficient" in an economic—if not in a human—sense.

In short, stirrings, connections, proposals, but no major action can be seen on the horizon.

9

Social Services for All?

ORDINARY people in the United States are being deprived of constructive solutions to problems in daily living, to those "normal" problems that arise out of societal change. Indeed, the term "problems" is probably inaccurate, since the programs involved represent appropriate, accepted responses to widely shared experience. The lag will get worse and we will pay a price unless we can offer a more hospitable environment to social invention.

We must begin by facing ideological blocks. Programs and benefits should and can be available to average people to meet normal living needs. They must be organized by both government and the voluntary sector (profit and nonprofit) so as to achieve social objectives other than those of the marketplace. The United States has some social services for all people. We need to become more comfortable in facing their normalcy if we are to improve and expand the components. Certainly such services for members of all social classes are no less essential to a society than the more traditional public welfare underpinnings for the poor and the deviant. Certainly this is no less attractive morally than governmental incentives, supports, and rescue operations for the business sector. All are, or can be, guided by shared overviews of the public interest and launched through democratic political process.

We believe in public education, yet we somehow cannot give public support to high-quality community living and care arrangements for the aged. We apparently consider it legitimate, whether in the interests of the economy or of equality of the sexes, to open broader opportunities for women in the labor force, yet we do not face rapidly and thoughtfully the need for a parallel child-care policy, fearing apparently that its outcome will be to "federalize" the children. We bemoan

171

alienation and drug addiction in young people, yet we make no serious large-scale efforts to offer wholesome living arrangements for them when they are away from their families. Only in recreation have we made headway; for about a century we have provided free, low-cost, and expensive summer camps for city children from all social classes.

Part of the rationale behind such half-measures and inconsistency is stated in the December 10, 1971, veto message in which President Nixon rejected large-scale child-development legislation:

All other factors being equal, good public policy requires that we enhance rather than diminish parental authority and parental involvement with children—particularly in those decisive years when social attitudes and a conscience are formed and religious and moral principles are first inculcated. . . . For the federal government to plunge headlong into supporting child development would commit the vast moral authority of the national government to the side of communal approaches to child rearing over against the family-centered approach.

This president, this government, is unwilling to take that step.

What the Europeans apparently know but what many Americans do not yet perceive is that social services may support, strengthen, enhance the normal family—and that failures in social provision may undermine our most precious institutions and relationships. The issue is not whether or not government will intervene. It will. The question is will it intervene for enhancement and prevention or to respond to breakdown, problems, and deviance alone. Will we create a sufficient supply of *public social utilities*, as we seek to create a supply of other public utilities? Or will we limit public provision to rescue operations, *case services*, helping and therapeutic arrangements for those in difficulty? Will we continue to pretend that only the "inadequate" need the services or face the universality of new social circumstances?

Whether programs foster dependency depends upon how they are administered and the nature of the entitlements. Are they beneficence, charity, given upon condition of subservience to those defined as weak? Or are they rights, seen as meeting widespread need, delivered with dignity, to a user who is seen as citizen, taxpayer, and policymaker? They need not be free services: minimum fees, graduated fees, partial fees are easily arranged for those with funds. College tuition may cover only 40 or 50 percent of costs—or be very, very low—yet no college student feels that he is a public assistance client.

It needs to be said more often, and understood by more people, that the assignment of general tax revenues for social programs is morally no different—if the services are in the public interest—from tax revenue for roads, canals, guns, or forest-fire fighting. Each social program can be analyzed to assure that payment methods and eligibility rules create the incentives, entitlements, and participation which our society chooses. Whether government programs create independence or dependence—or, for that matter, whether they create urban amenity, a sense of fairness, and dedication to one's neighborhood and peers—will depend upon how they are done, by whom and for whom, how they are administered and how paid for. Why ignore all of this in the debate about government?

Yet we fear to experiment, to discuss, and to consider the consequences. In all of this we preserve some myths, justify some suffering and deprivation, and avoid facing social realities. The posture may appear to save money but it also reinforces costly inequities and creates a less attractive society for every one of us. It is a policy which undercuts unnecessarily the living standards both of working people and of the middle class. If we really look at the daily lives of children, young people, houseparents, workers, and old people—in short, of all Americans, whether living in families or living on their own—we will not sustain such a policy.

Trends

This is not the place for a full tract on social trends, but a few illustrations may suggest the urgency of the message. We direct the spotlight toward everyone, the universal experience, *not* to the sick, the poor, the troubled, the deviant.

The dependency ratio in the United States has gone up. Together, those considered too young for the labor market (under eighteen) and those encouraged to stop work (over sixty-four) constitute 44 percent of the population. In 1950, they constituted 39 percent. Put differently, in 1973 the average American family had 3.5 members, of whom 1.3 were under eighteen, 2.0 were eighteen to sixty-four, and 0.3 were over sixty-four. Society cannot sustain the inevitable needed, appropriate, biological dependency (the very youngest children), encourage more dependency (extended education in the young), and indeed mandate it (retirement at a time when body and mind are still willing) without giving each type of dependency institutional form and the required benefits and program budgets. Nor will we do well unless each category, while perhaps economically and in some sense physically dependent, is permitted to develop a socially respected role which, in turn, enhances development, socialization, and social contributions.

While retirees and preschoolers constitute a larger population bloc and pose a clear challenge, opportunities in the marketplace, a quest for equality, and the decline of domestic farm labor have taken many women in the productive ages into the labor force, where once they worked at home or on farms, or were dependent members of a leisure class. Mothers of many young children now work full time. The number of children with working mothers increased by 650,000 between 1970 and 1973 (at a time when there were 1.5 million fewer children in families). Of 64.3 million children under eighteen in March 1973, 26.2 million had mothers in the labor force. Some 6 million of these children were under age six (almost one-third of all children under six). Of those mothers with children under six, 45 percent worked; of those whose children were six to seventeen years old, 57 percent worked. Nor are the female workers largely unmarried, separated, divorced, or widowed. Half of all wives (50.5 percent) living in households with husbands present worked during 1972. The rate was almost as high for white wives alone (49.6 percent). Even those with children under three are increasingly in the labor force (29 percent in March 1973). Wives with children three to five years of age and with no children under three are even more likely to be at work (38.3 percent). In short, ever larger numbers of mothers of young children work all year round, full time, and the trend line is up. Society cannot ignore the question of who takes care of the younger children.

The labor market picture does not exhaust the child-care question. Some even question any effort to associate the issues. There are many women who do not hold jobs who think it good for their children to have group experiences and good for themselves to have opportunity for other activity. Besides, many Americans feel that those mothers of young children who are receiving financial assistance should place their children in daytime care, take training, and work. We would also like to offer programs to children from deprived backgrounds, most of them members of ethnic and racial minorities, on the assumption that such programs will overcome the consequences of deprivation. In short, the rearing of very young children has ceased to be a household monopoly.

While American day-care supply data are incomplete and outdated, there is widespread evidence of shortages in many places. Long-term needs will be even greater if projected labor-force trends and changes in women's roles continue. (In Swedish terms, the equality movement has hardly begun in the United States.) Moreover, evidence is available of considerable below-standard daytime care of infants, very young children, and school-age children and even of noncare, despite increased American investment in several categories of early childhood programs: day care, Head Start, preschool programs in the school system for deprived children, private nonprofit nursery schools, proprietary day care, publicly subsidized family day care, franchises, and so on. Moreover what exists is costly and often has disappointing results. The excessive program and child categorizations are exasperating and the programing debate intensive. It is a movement needing new direction. And yet there remain those who would "abolish" it.

For the aged, the United States has concentrated on income security and health coverage, and has made progress despite major scandals and disappointments. Noting that there are now more than 21 million Americans aged sixty-five and over—and that by 1980 there will be 24 million, over 10 percent of the total population—and that many will be isolated and unable to manage without some help, U.S. policymakers have begun to face the obvious questions: Where will they live? What services will they need? What do they want? Are some programs more effective, more humane, cheaper? Can we do better than the reported horrors of some 23,000 private nursing homes, largely publicly supported at a cost of $4.5 billion annually?[1] Most people retire at sixty-five. In 1940, life expectancy at birth was 60.8 years for men and 65.2 years for women. By 1973 it had become 67.4 years for men, 74.9 years for women. The questions, in short, pertain to the welfare of large numbers of average Americans over significant proportions of their lifetimes.

One further illustration. In 1974, a census expert told a Senate subcommittee: "Particularly impressive has been the rapid increase over the past decade in the number of young adults who have been maintaining their own households apart from relatives." It would be difficult to find an expert who would not agree that in cities throughout the country there are thousands of such young adults who lack satisfactory living arrangements. Except for the YMCA and YWCA hotels, whose roles are declining, and for a limited number of other facilities, there are few who attempt to meet this need.

But there is a stronger, more central trend: we cannot but wonder about the quality of child life, family life, life in the retirement years, as we note the decline in large households and the shift of family tasks to other institutions and as we observe the limited resources of some

---

1. Susan Gray, "Waiting for the End: On Nursing Homes," *New York Times Magazine*, March 31, 1974.

families in coping with all this. Supermarket and laundry room replace the "big kitchen" and the telephone cuts distances and facilitates a new style of "visiting" and relationship. Yet it is hardly clear that the needs of young children or old people get adequate attention in the family time-and-money "budget." Does the family need to be further strengthened in its new tasks, featuring nurture, socialization, development, emotional satisfactions?

There are, after all, more separations, divorces, remarriages, unmarrieds "living together" than before. Young people leave home to work elsewhere in the country—or just to live more independently. Relatives are sometimes far from young couples. Family members have less time together.

The concern with these and similar trends is premised on the assumption that family life is good for developing children or retired old people and that, therefore, family life should in some way be approximated, and strengthened, as it shifts its specific character. Or, in the absence of a "full family" or traditional family forms, those individuals who are living apart—or together—should be assured family-like social supports, or at least what sociologists call "primary group" experience. Nor is the case one of social altruism: society has interest in the ultimate environment which gives sustenance to individuals because society has a stake in mental health, social adjustment, the quality of life, the caliber of its growing generations. Even those who fear excessive involvement cannot argue against a floor, a minimum, a protected border, if only for the children.

Policy

The response will be inadequate if it is limited to noting needs and creating specific programs to meet them. Such remedial, serial, incremental (and often grudging) acknowledgement ignores the need for plan, choice, and coherence.

The observer of domestic policy developments in Western societies recognizes many difficult issues. Communities need public services, even some social services available to all, but these must be balanced against personal disposable income. If given a choice, American citizens, at least, do not vote for "in kind" benefits until they have a minimum of cash. Many Americans also prefer that the retired, the disabled, and the poor also have some cash. Similarly, despite acknowledged need for services which make it possible for old people to continue their lives in the community and not in closed institutions, as long as possible, there is also need for basic medical services; indeed, money, medical care, and housing policy are the foundation of all living and care arrangements.

One should not think only of the aged, however, ignoring the children; or only of the retired, ignoring the housewife. Personal social services should not develop at the expense of education, or housing arrangements at the expense of manpower and employment.

These are all limited and illustrative comments. Domestic social programs, while not completely indivisible, have major interdependencies and constraints. They also face resource realities. There are issues of balance. Thus, to deploy resources strategically and in a specific sequence, there is need for continuing research and discussion, to define preferences and needs, and for planning, to assure optimal resource deployment at appropriate times and in desirable interrelationships. If this is to be productive, imagination and innovation must be encouraged.

Government and voluntary social welfare agencies do some things to and for families deliberately and specifically: day care, general social services such as child welfare and family counseling, income maintenance, family planning, some tax benefits, some housing activities, and so forth. These may be thought of as a subcategory of overall social policy: *explicit family policy*. There are also many activities, policies, and programs which are addressed to other targets but which affect families. The family impacts may be visible, predicted but secondary to the primary objective, or they may be unintended or even unrecognized impacts—unrecognized, that is, until felt and investigated. These are elements of *implicit family policy*: tax law, housing programs, trade and tariff regulations, road building, industrial location decisions, working hours, the organization of medical practice (to offer a partial listing).

Out of respect for our traditions and legitimate concern that damage not be done to our fundamental institutions, family policy has not been discussed or debated much in the United States. In fact, when the phrase is used many think that it refers only to population policy or to family planning. Clearly there is a gap between social change and social policies in this realm. Americans have a stake in making the needs, problems, risks, and alternatives visible. We need a family policy debate in the context of our overall domestic social policy explorations. It should be as open, widespread, and heated (but as serious about trends, needs, alternatives) as Sweden's equality discussion. It belongs within the domestic political process and can only benefit from adequate attention there. A few voices have recently been heard in that debate (see For Further Reading) but the range of content is narrow and the volume low.

The United States has not, of course, stood completely still. In each chapter, where American connections are made, we have noted our progress. People in this country have applied dedication and imagination to child care, community facilities for the aging, school meals, health services, residences, and other essential areas. Nothing described lacks an excellent American counterpart, somewhere. But we in the United States have problems of coverage, quality, eligibility, and program aura (stigma or privilege?). These problems will remain unless we also deal more systematically with issues of policy and commitment.

Optimism about long-term prospects may be built on the record of social innovation, on available precedent, and on the knowledge that if a program is a good one, it is utilized. Encouragement also may be taken from the recognition by private enterprise that there are social programs so essential and so responsive to widespread need that they may even do well in the marketplace. (We refer to franchise day care, proprietary residential communities for the aged, commercial housing for the single, and so on. Here the problem is coverage, eligibility, and the balance between money-making and program quality.) Moreover, as industrial productivity increases everywhere, more and more members of the labor force are eligible for employment in the service sector, both profit and nonprofit. There will be personnel to man the services if we can decide how to pay for them. Finally, the need for social services—a specialized segment of the service sector—is increasingly recognized. Humane impulses have increased somewhat the public commitment to case services, the helping and therapeutic-rehabilitative social service programs for the troubled, hurt, deviant. Now similar investment is needed in *public social utilities*, basic services for average people in response to daily needs.

Recognition of need expands and is seen daily in the media, but just how potent that recognition has become is not yet fully clear. Reporter E. J. Kahn, interpreter of the U.S. census, has noted in the *New Yorker* (October 22, 1973, p. 122) that by 1970, in Tunica County, Mississippi, the poorest county in the poorest state in the United States, 61 percent of households had washing machines, 61 percent had cars, and 86 percent had television sets. Ours is a luxury-loving, high-consumption society. Ultimately there must be a balance between increasing the distribution of such factory-built amenities—or converting to color TVs and new cars—or enjoying trips, restaurants, better clothing—and the costs of more extensive social programs. We do not expect the American taxpayer to vote "yes" for even a very modest decrease of personal disposable income in exchange for social services unless he believes that his own life, and the lives of his parents and children, will be enriched thereby. We doubt that he will do it out of charity for the deviant and unfortunate, whatever the average level of generosity in the society. But we also believe that the argument for self-interest looms large.

The aged, the mothers, the unattached young people, the children, the families of whom we have written here are by no means only the poor, the deviant, the troubled, of our societies. They are everyman— and are increasingly recognized as such. Domestic social policy and social invention would do well to attend to this fact. Explorations of developments in several European countries suggest that without ending democracy, individual initiative, or personal responsibility, government can contribute to amenity, enriched living, and social integration—and that all of us might benefit from the process.

The word "welfare" is often reserved in the United States for the public assistance recipients, the "welfare" poor. Elsewhere, in the "welfare state" context (why not the "consumer" or "service" state?), it has a deeper meaning. Since we have referred, among others, to Swedish programs, which expand despite costs, we end with a quotation from Sweden's prime minister:

> We have to show the viability of the welfare state . . . , show that democracy can handle it. We must stand or fall in an industrial society. We can't do away with it or we'd be back in the Middle Ages. We are trying to renew it from within.
> Society is about homes, people, their loneliness and their need of community with others. The trouble is we have still too little welfare permeating society.

Many Americans are afraid of words such as these and are often turned away from needed programs by them. But we, too, have needs: homes, income, services, problems, loneliness, community. . . .

For Further Reading

Anderson, Oden W. *Health Care: Can There Be Equality?* New York: John Wiley & Sons, 1972.

American Families: Trends and Pressures, 1973. Hearings before the Subcommittee on Children and Youth of the Committee on Labor and Welfare, U.S. Senate, September, 1973. Washington, D.C.: U.S. Government Printing Office, 1974.

Berfanstam, Ragmar, and Inger William-Olsson. *Early Child Care in Sweden.* London: Gordon & Breach, 1973.

Bronfenbrenner, Urie. *Two Worlds of Childhood: U.S. and U.S.S.R.* New York: Russell Sage Foundation, 1970. (Distributed by Basic Books.)

Burns, Eveline, ed., *Children's Allowances and the Economic Welfare of Children.* New York: Citizens Committee for Children, 1968.

Clapp, James A. *New Towns and Urban Policy.* New York: Dunellen, 1971.

Cohen, Donald M., M.D. *Serving Preschool Children.* Office of Child Development, DHEW Publication No. (OHD) 74–1057. Washington, D.C.: U.S. Government Printing Office, 1974.

Community/School: Sharing the Space and the Action. New York: Educational Facilities Laboratories, 1973.

Kahn, Alfred J. *Social Policy and Social Services.* New York: Random House, 1973.

Myrdal, Alva. *Nation and Family.* Cambridge, Mass.: M.I.T. Press, 1968. (Paperback ed., including Foreword by Daniel P. Moynihan.)

Perloff, Harvey S., and Neil C. Sandberg, eds. *New Towns: Why and for Whom.* New York: Praeger, 1973.

Robson, William A., and Bernard Crick. *The Future of the Social Services.* London: Penguin Books, 1970.

Schorr, Alvin. *Poor Kids.* New York: Basic Books, 1966.

Steinfels, Margaret O'Brien. *Who's Minding the Children.* New York: Simon & Schuster, 1973.

Towards Equality: The Alva Myrdal Report to the Swedish Social Democratic Party. Stockholm: Prisma Publishers, 1971.

Trager, Brahna. *Home Health Services in the United States.* A Report for the Special Committee on Aging, U.S. Senate. Washington, D.C.: U.S. Government Printing Office, 1972.

U.S. Department of Health, Education, and Welfare, Office of Research and Statistics, Social Security Administration. *Social Security throughout the World, 1973.* Washington, D.C.: U.S. Government Printing Office, 1974.

Young, Dennis R., and Richard R. Nelson. *Public Policy for Day-Care of Young Children.* Lexington, Mass.: D. C. Heath, 1973. (Lexington Book Series.)

The following Swedish Institute pamphlets in English are available through Swedish government offices in the U.S.: *Social Benefits in Sweden* (revised annually), *Pre-School in Sweden* (1972), *Public Health in Sweden* (1972). Or write to the Swedish Institute, Box 7072, 103–82 Stockholm 7, Sweden.

Index

Creativity in Social Work

Selected Writings of Lydia Rapoport

Edited by SANFORD N. KATZ

Introduction by Carol H. Meyer
Foreword by Dame Eileen Younghusband

Lydia Rapoport's pioneering efforts in crisis intervention, short-term therapy, and family planning are amply documented in this collection of her most influential writings. Her dedication to the value and dignity of social work and her ability to combine theory with practice make this essential reading for both the practitioner and the student.

"Viewed as a whole, these writings of Lydia Rapoport present a method for becoming an effective, intellectual professional practitioner, aiming toward high standards, maintaining relevance to the current social realities, and aware of future possibilities."—From the Introduction by Carol H. Meyer

Perspectives in Social Casework

HELEN HARRIS PERLMAN

In this increasingly faceless society, serving individuals in personal need has a unique value. An experienced professional delineates the special identity of casework and its place within social work as a whole. "One of the most articulate and readable interpreters of social work known to our profession."—Lola G. Selby, *Social Service Review*

The Rights of Children

Emergent Concepts in Law and Society

Edited by ALBERT E. WILKERSON

Introduction by Justine Wise Polier

"A well-organized gathering of the sometimes clashing views of a wide range of this country's most respected judges, legislators, social workers, and lawyers. Their focus is on existing conditions affecting children's rights and lives, and on social and legal concepts making news today."
—*Publishers Weekly*

Temple University Press

Philadelphia